ALONG THE SHADOW LINE

The Fall of Richmond, Va. on the night of April 2, 1865.
Originally published by Currier & Ives, c. 1865. Courtesy of LOC.

Along The Shadow Line

A Road Trip Through History and
Memory on the Old Confederate Border

H. V. Traywick, Jr.

"It's all now you see. Yesterday won't be over until tomorrow and tomorrow began ten thousand years ago."

— William Faulkner, from *Intruder in the Dust*

Along The Shadow Line: A Road Trip through History and Memory on the Old Confederate Border

Copyright© 2024 by H. V. Traywick, Jr.

ALL RIGHTS RESERVED. No part of this publication may be reproduced, distributed, or transmitted in any form or by any means, including photocopying, recording, or other electronic or mechanical methods, or by any information storage and retrieval system without the prior written permission of the publisher, except in the case of very brief quotations embodied in critical reviews and certain other non-commercial uses permitted by copyright law.

Produced in the Republic of South Carolina by

SHOTWELL PUBLISHING LLC

Post Office Box 2592

Columbia, So. Carolina 29202

www.ShotwellPublishing.com

Cover Design by Boo Jackson

ISBN: 978-1-963506-00-6

FIRST EDITION

10 9 8 7 6 5 4 3 2 1

Dedicated to the memory of
Robert William Grantham,
Sailor on a Concrete Sea

Smart lad, to slip betimes away

From fields where glory does not stay,

And early though the laurel grows

It withers quicker than the rose...

— A. E. Housman

Contents

Acknowledgements IX

Author's Note: On Lines And Shadows XI

Introduction: On A Kansas Prairie By Mary Luby XIII

Foreword: On The Shadow Line..................................XV

I. Virginia 1

II. West Virginia 17

III. Kentucky 25

IV. Indiana 33

V. Illinois..41

VI. Missouri..49

VII. Kansas...61

VIII. Beyond 63

About The Author..67

Acknowledgements

THANKS MUST GO TO my cousin Mary, my little playmate of childhood, who has offered me her generous Kansas hospitality in my trips out to her ranch. She is also an accomplished writer, published author, and English teacher who has graciously given of her very busy schedule with the relentless daily demands of tending to forty or fifty dogs, to review my manuscript, correct my text, and offer helpful suggestions on composition—including the sub-title. The work is much better for it. The lapses are all my own.

I wish to sincerely thank my publishers, Dr. Clyde Wilson and Shotwell Publishing, for their professional work in bringing this out, and who have undertaken this work with courage in the face of those many who might take issue with it in these turbulent times.

Author's Note

On Lines And Shadows

GEOMETRICALLY, A LINE IS AN INFINITE number of points. It can be an artificial construct, such as a latitude or a longitude, or naturally occurring, such as the shoreline of a lake, a river, or the sea. Lines mark boundaries. Boundary lines of countries can be sharp and settled, such as the border between the United States and Canada, or vague and contested as battles rage over them. In my travels back and forth between Virginia and Kansas, my route took me along such a line that once ran between two countries at war — the United States of America and the storm-tossed Southern Confederacy — a line that runs up the Potomac River, across the mountains, down the Ohio River, across the Mississippi, and up the Missouri to Kansas.

Lines can be not only spatial, but spiritual and temporal as well. In Joseph Conrad's novella *The Shadow-Line*, he says, "Yes. One goes on. And the time, too, goes on — till one perceives ahead a shadow-line warning one that the region of early youth, too, must be left behind." In this rambling account of my travels from Virginia to Kansas, I take note of many lines — some sharp, some not, some on the map, some not, some spatial, some temporal, and some in shadows on the edge of reality — ever mindful of the shadow-line that awaits me on the road up ahead.

H. V. Traywick, Jr.

Richmond, Virginia

Introduction

On A Kansas Prairie
By Mary Luby

WHEN MY HUSBAND died unexpectedly in 2022, I found myself bereft without him and alone on 50 acres on a Kansas prairie, or alone as one can be with the company of multiple dogs.

I was an Easterner at heart as my mother hailed from Virginia and I was born in Washington, DC. But I was a Navy junior and thus a tumbleweed which aided in my ability to adjust to an alien land in my 40s when my first husband, daughter and I moved to Kansas, a "flyover" State.

I am one of seven first cousins from my mother's side. I never met anyone from my father's family in New York. My favorite cousin, Bo, and I were the same age and spent long, hot summers playing in our grandparents' yard in Virginia when I visited between moving hither and yon. We tormented our parents by running and hiding in the woods when it was time for me to move yet again, and we never grew out of being "difficult," as my mother would say. Being a direct descendent of the Knight of Melrose, Bo felt a call to arms when he heard of my plight and packed his bags, sword and shield, and headed to the Kansas prairie.

A year later, after he had gone back and forth to Virginia to take care of "things," we were sitting on the deck one evening. With the endless waving pastures of tall prairie grass behind us and the waning Kansas sun disappearing on the horizon, he shared an idea for a memoir of sorts, a chronology of his travels to the plains, and the memories it brought back of his ancestors and those men that fought in gray.

These stories would stem from the journey Bo would take, leading him through the halls of history from the Civil War to now, a time of chaos in our saddened country. This would be a journey in his later years, leaving him to reflect upon his life and its meaning, and introduce him to heretofore unknown regions of our land. Having spent years on the East Coast, the Chesapeake Bay and the Atlantic Ocean as a tugboat captain, and as a trawler captain along the Carolina and Georgia coasts, he had never truly traveled the Midwest. In mapping out his trip, he realized he would be traveling on the borders of the Civil War States. Being an accomplished historian of the War Between the States, he reminisced on his journey about the war, its outcome, and how the South paid the price for men of ambition.

*

Foreword

On The Shadow Line

And them that had escaped from the sword carried he away to Babylon...   —II Chronicles 36:20

BEFORE DAYLIGHT ON A MORNING in early April, Captain Clement Sulivane and his infantry detachment were posted on the last bridge out of Richmond. As he waited for Gary's South Carolina cavalry to arrive he watched the burning city and the rushing waters of the old James River. Lee's lines had been broken below Petersburg and the army was in full retreat towards Danville. Richmond was being evacuated and the tobacco warehouses had been ordered to be set afire. As the heat swelled the prized tobacco it caused the bands to burst on the hogsheads, and the burning tobacco leaves showered over the city and spread the fires. As the arsenal caught fire, powder magazines began exploding in deafening roars that rocked the city, columns of smoke blew heavenward as bursting artillery shells sent their iron missiles high into the air and showering down into the sparkling river below amidst the rattle of thousands of ignited musket cartridges. The guards had been removed from the commissary depot and hungry mobs swarmed the streets, some lapping whiskey that ran in the gutters, for Richmond was a starving city. Captain Sulivane, gazing upon the horrific splendor of the scene, was witnessing the death and destruction of the "Mother of States and Statesmen."

In 1607, three ships appeared off Cape Henry out of an immensity that, as Joseph Conrad said, "receives no impress, preserves no memories, and keeps no reckoning of lives." Men went ashore and planted a cross. From there they sailed into Chesapeake Bay past

Old Point Comfort and up the James River, where they planted the first permanent English settlement in the New World at Jamestown Island. By 1619 representative government had been established, women had arrived, tobacco had been planted, and the first cargo of twenty Africans were purchased as indentured servants from a Dutch man o' war to help with the cultivation, long before the Pilgrims ever set foot on Plymouth Rock in New England. Virginia prospered and great plantations sprang up along the Tidewater rivers, while frontiersmen pushed to the mountains and beyond until the colony extended westward to the Mississippi and northwestward to the Great Lakes. In 1775 troubles with England broke out into open warfare in the New England colonies and a Virginia planter named George Washington marched a contingent of Virginians northward to their relief, eventually becoming Commander-in-Chief of the Continental Army. A Virginia planter named Thomas Jefferson wrote The Declaration of Independence as the war spread southward throughout the thirteen colonies. With the indispensable aid of France, it ended with the colonies' independence at Yorktown, Virginia. Thereafter a confederation of the thirteen newly independent States was established. George Washington was named President and "The Father of His Country," while a Virginia planter named James Madison was credited with being "The Father of the Constitution" — the charter of the new Republic. This Constitution granted limited, enumerated powers to a small central government, and guaranteed all the residuary powers to the respective States and to the people therein. Virginia voluntarily gave up her Northwest empire to this new Union and provided four of its first five presidents — all of whom were planters. But with the coming of the Industrial Revolution trouble arose between the industrializing Northern States and the agrarian Southern States. When the Southern States attempted to peacefully withdraw from the Union at the election of Abraham Lincoln and his radical and strictly sectional Northern political party, the North invaded the Southern States to drive them back into the Union at the point of the bayonet. After four years of warfare, it had now come down to this....

Foreword

The flames of the city came closer and closer and at last caught fire to the commissariat itself. At daylight, the approach of Union troops into the city could be plainly seen and the picket across the canal was withdrawn. By order of the Engineer Department, tar barrels surrounded by fat pine-knots with kerosene at hand were placed at intervals on the bridge in preparation for firing. A Lieutenant of Engineers stood by with a lighted pine-knot torch ready on orders to apply the flame. The hoof beats of Gary's ambulance train were heard turning down for the bridge, but the muleteers were stopped by the seething mob. Captain Sulivane rode forward and cleared the way and the ambulances rushed for the bridge. A few minutes later a long line of cavalry followed with their sabres drawn and scattered the mob. Gary had come. His troopers reigned up waiting for the rear guard who rushed headlong for the bridge. Then Gary, touching his hat to the captain, said, "All over, good-bye; blow her to hell," and trotted over the bridge.

*

I.

Virginia

Oh, Shenandoah, I'm bound to leave you,

Away, you rolling river

Oh, Shenandoah, I'm bound to leave you,

Away, I'm bound away, across the wide Missouri.

I WAS SADDENED AND DISTRESSED TO HEAR the news of Terry's passing. Terry was an accomplished and highly respected CPA in Kansas who had seemed to be in perfect health. Many times he rode the famous Triple Bypass bike marathon, 135 miles through the highest mountain passes in Colorado, completed two Ironman competitions, and literally hundreds of running marathons, setting a standard of excellence for all of us, so the news came as a shock. But against Mary's earnest remonstrations, he had insisted on taking the Covid shots and boosters for the sake of his clients, although he already had natural immunity. Complications immediately ensued, with the loss of the use of his legs, heart issues, and blindness. Local medical facilities were a travesty, and he was sent home with pneumonia and a high fever. Again, in the hospital and suffering on a ventilator, he departed this earth and its travails. Mary's lawyer said trying to sue for medical neglect and malpractice would bankrupt her, so she was left alone with anger, devastation, and a fifty-acre dog rescue ranch to manage.

When I heard the news, I drove back out there to see if I could help her settle the estate and do whatever I could. It was a long way from our grandparents' front yard, running barefooted through the lush bluegrass in the endless summers, or building little twig houses between the roots of the great oaks for our little glass animals, or picking the little flowers we called "blueys" that grew in the grass, or catching lightning bugs in the balmy evenings, or raking paths in the fall leaves. But things run in cycles, and as The Preacher says,

> *All the rivers run into the sea; yet the sea is not full; unto the place from whence the rivers come, thither they return again.* — Ecclesiastes 1:7

So I saddled up and left Richmond, bound west. My route would take me parallel to an old line of demarcation on the maps of history that marked the northern frontier of the old Southern Confederacy, a shadow-line today that roughly runs from the Chesapeake Bay, up the Potomac, across the mountains, down the Ohio, across the Mississippi, and up the Missouri to Kansas. My travels — with my rambling observations, thoughts on history, and memories recorded along the way — would be along Interstate 64 from Virginia, through West Virginia, Kentucky, Indiana, and Illinois to St. Louis, and from there through Missouri to Kansas on I-70.

Leaving home, I first crossed to the north side of the James River on the Powhite Parkway Bridge. There is a Powhite Creek nearby, which gives the bridge its name. The creek itself, I suppose, got its name from "Po' Whites" who had lived along it "back in the day." I can only imagine if a like Black pejorative were given as the name of a bridge. Newscasters would be clutching their pearls, politicians would be proclaiming their outrage across the airwaves, and race hustlers would be in their glory as a pandemic of apoplexy and rioting swept the land.

Below the bridge are rapids, for Richmond is on the fall line, which is the James River's head of navigation. The Fall Line separates the flat lands of Tidewater from the rolling hills of the Piedmont. The

Deepwater Terminal is below town off Interstate 95 where tugs bring container barges up from Norfolk, and across the Interstate is the cigarette manufacturing company Altria, which makes Richmond still a tobacco town.

Tobacco is grown on contract these days, so the old tobacco auction houses of Southside have disappeared. In fact, one rarely sees a tobacco field anymore. I saw a large one on US 360 in Charlotte County recently, and I have seen several in North Carolina along I-95, but the broad fields I remember below Lynchburg on the way to Danville are rare, and the old tobacco barns are collapsing and disappearing in honeysuckle and kudzu. But once tobacco was grown in the streets of Jamestown and the leaves were used as money. It became the staple crop of Virginia until it began to "wear out the soil." Farms and plantations lapsed into weeds and people began to move west — the farmers to Kentucky, Tennessee, the Ohio River valley, and Missouri, and the planters to the new cotton lands of Alabama and Mississippi.

But one planter stayed. Edmund Ruffin, who fired the first and last shots of the War for Southern Independence, was not only a planter but a soil scientist. He realized that the "worn out" tobacco lands grew pine trees and broom straw abundantly, and after researching the still-flourishing wheat lands of the Shenandoah Valley he noted the prevalence of limestone in the soil there. He determined — correctly — that tobacco had not worn out the land but had changed the *ph* of the soil from sweet to acid. He went home to his plantation and had his people dig the clayey marl from the riverbanks and spread it on the land. His crops began to flourish dramatically, and he wrote of his discovery in his book entitled *An Essay on Calcareous Manures*. It is not exactly what one might call a "gripping page-turner," but it put Old Virginia on the verge of restoring her ancient prosperity just before the war broke out. Edmund Ruffin rests at his old plantation — still a working farm and still in the family — on a bluff overlooking the land that he had cared for so well.

There is no new thing under the sun, as the Scriptures tell us. The land is eternal, we are its stewards, and the ancient wisdom of the Laws of Moses directing that the land shall have a Sabbath of rest still applies, for farmers now rotate crops and allow land to lie fallow:

> *Six years thou shalt sow thy field, and six years thou shalt prune thy vineyard, and gather in the fruit thereof; But in the seventh year shall be a Sabbath of rest unto the land, a Sabbath for the Lord...*
> — Leviticus 25:3-4

According to these Ancient Scriptures, this, and not slavery, was our "original sin." The fiftieth year, the famous Year of Jubilee following seven Sabbaths of the land, where "every man is to be returned to his possession," appears in the Laws of Moses to apply only to indentured servants, not slaves. According to Leviticus 25:44-46, the bondmen, or slaves, shall be ...

> *of the strangers that do sojourn among you, of them shall you buy ... And ye shall take them as an inheritance for your children after you, to inherit them as a possession; they shall be your bondmen for ever...*

When the children of Israel were carried away into Babylon, it was not because of their not releasing their slaves in the Year of Jubilee (which the Law did not prescribe) but

> *To fulfil the word of the Lord by the mouth of Jeremiah, until the land had enjoyed her Sabbaths: for as long as she lay desolate she kept Sabbath, to fulfil threescore and ten years.* — II Chronicles 36:21

Threescore and ten years was the same length of time that the South lay desolate after the war.

A little ways above Richmond's Deepwater Terminal is Rocketts Landing in Shockoe Bottom. In the old days there was a slave market there known as "Lumpkin's Slave Jail," or "Hell's Half-acre." In colonial times, Virginia tried to stop the traffic from Africa but the English Crown forbade it. Trading rum and trinkets to African Kings for the slaves they held for sale in their barracoons on the beach was a booming business not only for the Crown, but for the African Kings, the European and New England slave-traders, and the sugar colonies of the Caribbean as well. After independence, however, Virginia was the first country in the world to prohibit the African Slave-trade.

The traffic was prohibited by the United States Constitution in 1808, but New England shippers carried on an illegal trade to Cuba and Brazil right up to the War Between the States. It was a triangular trade, with rum distilled in New England from slave-harvested sugar cane carried to the West African coast for barter for slaves, then the transport of slaves in the dreadful "middle passage" to the sugar colonies of the Caribbean, and finally the transport of sugar back to New England for its distillation into rum. Slaves were packed like sardines and chained below decks in sweltering holds amid excrement and filth. The bodies of those that died were dumped overboard without ceremony. It was said that a slaver could be smelled from a mile down wind.

The New England trade started within twenty years of the arrival of the Pilgrims and the money from it soon built the mansions of Newport and elsewhere and endowed Ivy League schools. The founder of Brown University, John Brown, (not *the* John Brown), said he saw no more problem in carrying off a cargo of Africans than in carrying off a cargo of jackasses. The January 1862 issue of the New York *Continental Monthly* (available online) reported that New York, Boston and Portland were the largest African Slave-trading ports in the world at the time of Abraham Lincoln's election. The wealth of Radical Abolitionist New England was founded on the African Slave-trade and on the manufacture and shipment of slave-picked cotton.

Although Virginia outlawed the African Slave-Trade immediately upon her independence, the domestic trade continued. As the Northern States found slavery inconvenient and uneconomical in their industrializing, urban, mercantile and small farm economy, they one by one abolished it. But, as Alexis de Tocqueville noted in his classic *Democracy in America*, they did not set their slaves free. Most were sold south before their State abolition laws went into effect. Markets in the Upper South, including Richmond, Fredericksburg, Alexandria, and Washington, DC, were the receivers of these slaves from the North. This is one reason why Virginia, in addition to being the oldest State in the Union, had the largest slave population of any before the war.

Virginia also had a large free Black population, for Southern abolitionists had been wrestling with the problems of ending slavery since before the Revolution. Many slaves were emancipated and resettled in Liberia, while many others remained in Virginia. James Curtis Ballagh, in his *A History of Slavery in Virginia*, estimated that Virginia planters by 1860 had manumitted one hundred thousand slaves, and without receiving a penny for doing so. Enough of these free Blacks were slave owners themselves to make the fact unremarkable at the time — a fact that is fervently swept under the rug today. A notable number of these free Black slave owners were large landowners and well-to-do planters. Dr. Carter G. Woodson, "The Father of Black History," enumerated the Black slave owners from the US Census in his book *Free Negro Owners of Slaves in the United States in 1830*. Though present from New Orleans to New England, they were mostly to be found in the older States of Maryland, Virginia, South Carolina and Louisiana.

It is interesting to note that the first actual slave owner in Virginia was a Black man. Anthony Johnson, who had been an indentured servant, worked off his indenture and owned a tobacco plantation on the Eastern Shore. For some reason he took one of his indentured servants to court to ask that the man be made "indentured for life," and the court ruled in his favor. That marked the true beginning of African slavery in British North America, not 1619.

At the head of navigation in the tidal basin at Richmond are a set of locks. These were built to lift vessels from the river into the James and Kanawha Canal. This canal was to provide transportation westward along the James and through the mountains to the Kanawha River, which empties into the Ohio River; but then came the railroads and canal construction was stopped somewhere in the mountains west of Lynchburg. Looking down from the Powhite Bridge one can see some of the remains of the canal. The railroad, which killed the canal, now uses the towpath in some places as its roadbed westward, but for my trip west I was using the even newer Interstate Highway System — which, along with television, air-conditioners and the internet, has scrambled us all.

Merging westbound onto I-64, one rolls along past the exits to Short Pump, one of the new upscale shopping areas of Richmond's western metropolitan region, then into Goochland and Louisa Counties. There one can make traveling speed through the lush greenery of the Eastern Hardwood Forest.

An hour west of Richmond is Charlottesville. Once a town of quiet academic dignity as the home of Mr. Jefferson's University, Jefferson has now been reviled as a Southern, slave-holding plantation owner, while Charlottesville has been branded by the media as a hotbed of White Supremacy with Klansmen lurking behind every bush and under every bed. This is the result of the rioting sparked by a Black race-hustler on the city council seeking to make a name for himself by advocating the removal of the equestrian statues of Generals Robert E. Lee and "Stonewall" Jackson. A rally was granted a permit to peacefully assemble and protest the removals, but the city ordered the Police to stand down while Antifa and Black Lives Matter mobs waded into the permitted rally. The rioting made the national news, of course, and made Charlottesville a byword for "White Supremacist Extremism." The monument issue was wrangled in court until they were finally taken down. I understand some group up there wants to grind up the statues and melt them into little trophies of some sort, most likely to be presented to "social justice warriors" as campaign ribbons.

Richmond was to go through the same drill during the George Floyd riots. A Black man named George Floyd, with a number of prior criminal convictions and with his system loaded with enough fentanyl to kill a horse, died under the restraining knee of a White police officer in Minneapolis, Minnesota, so it naturally followed that all the Confederate monuments in the South had to come down. In Richmond, Virginia Commonwealth University students and their "woke" fellow travelers (mostly White, by the footage shown on the newscasts) swarmed out Monument Avenue in a frenzied orgy of vandalism. (The VCU campus is near some housing projects, so it is evidently deemed prudent for the White students to demonstrate their "woke" virtues as self-preservation insurance.) Rioting was widespread downtown for days and business storefronts were trashed. On a boulevard nearby, the Headquarters of the United Daughters of the Confederacy was firebombed, and the sprinkler system that was set off ruined the priceless library. Organized Antifa and Black Lives Matter (BLM) "social justice warriors" were involved, with pre-positioned piles of brickbats placed strategically ahead of time. There were no arrests made that I ever heard of, but the police were brought to court for using tear gas.

Blacks kill Blacks on a regular basis on any weekend in big cities in the country, but to judge from the crickets heard from BLM, *those* "Black Lives" don't seem to "Matter." One might logically conclude from this that the killing of Blacks is considered by BLM to be a Black prerogative. BLM is an avowed Marxist organization, and, like the Southern Poverty Law Center, it is a lucrative racket for shaking down Desperate White Liberals.

Antifa has a Richmond chapter also, but they seem to have originated in the Pacific Northwest before George Floyd's "Summer of Love" riots. Andy Gno, who has written about them in his book entitled *Unmasked* and who has been beaten up by them, says "Most of Antifa's doxing and intimidation tactics skirt the line on criminality... Driven by intense hatred, Antifa want their targets to fear living a normal life. This is their terrorism without violence." Antifa consider themselves social justice warriors and "anti-fascists," but their fascist tactics brand them as being little different than Hitler's Brownshirts. As leftist "rent-a-thugs" they generally enjoy immunity from prosecution either under the law or in the media.

Richmond, now a Black-run city, took down the monuments on Monument Avenue with an out-of-State Black-owned crane company (no contractor in Richmond would touch them) and dumped them at the city's wastewater treatment plant with the city's promise to give them to the Black History Museum. Lee Circle, where the Lee Monument once stood, was informally re-named Marcus-David Peters Circle after a Black man who was shot by the police. Luckily for Richmond the officer who shot him was also Black. After the removal of the Lee Monument the circle had to be fenced off because of all the drug dealing going on around there. Residents in the stately homes on what is now "Monument-less" Avenue complained of gunfire and bullet holes and of people using their yards for a latrine. Meanwhile, the colossal equestrian statue of a Black "homeboy" adorned with dreadlocks by Black sculptor Kehinde Wiley entitled "Rumors of War," (he said he was inspired to mock General J. E. B. Stuart's equestrian monument), was erected amidst the orgasmic adulation of Desperate White Liberals in front of the Virginia Museum of Fine Arts — a fitting monument to our descent into the barbarism that "Jeb" Stuart had fought and died to prevent.

The Civil Rights Movement of the 1960s had romantic appeal. Television allowed the romantics to post their championship of the underdogs of society for all the world to see. Such romanticism swept the colleges and universities, and when Blacks got their full civil rights, subsequent young idealistic college students carried on the romance by finding other marginalized groups to champion. First came the "Feminists," then the "Abortion Rights" groups, followed by the "Gay Rights" crowd — whose discreet sexual behavior in the past was "brought out of the closet" so it could be shoved down everyone else's throats. Now Blacks, "minorities," Feminists, "Gays," and other "victims of society" band together in "intersectionality" to amplify their political clout.

As time goes by and more and more "oppressed minorities" get their evermore specious "civil rights," progressively more obscure groups have been brought forth to carry on the romance until we have come to the transgender movement, replete with hormone blockers, "Drag Queen Story Hour," and sex change mutilation of children; homoerotic pornography in middle school libraries; hulking biological men competing in women's swim meets and showering in the women's locker room in high schools and colleges; and Rainbow Pride parades with grown men prancing around naked in the streets and waving rainbow flags.

With LGBTQ+ now encompassing every oppressed minority under the sun, there seems to be nothing left for the Civil Rights romantics and the social justice warriors to do but to drum up White Supremacy, White terrorism and Western Civilization as "the enemy of the people," which brings us to something straight out of *The Communist Manifesto* or Chairman Mao's *Little Red Book*. The "Deep State" and their handmaidens in the media have obligingly lit the way for these "useful idiots" by lighting Reichstag Fires from Charlottesville to January 6.

LaFayette, we are gone; Robespierre, we are here. We have crossed the shadow-line into an Orwellian nightmare.

Beyond Charlottesville is Afton Mountain, on the ramparts of the Blue Ridge. There are signs with flashing yellow lights giving warnings of fog or sometimes ice on the mountain in changing weather. The road widens to three lanes so the big trucks can make the climb in their lower gears without impeding other traffic, and they are prohibited from using the leftmost lane. Near the top of the mountain there is an open vista of breathtaking beauty that extends far away into the misty southwest.

Crossing the peak, there is a sign indicating that you are entering the Shenandoah Valley Battlefields National Historic District. This is the upper end of the Valley of Virginia and there was much fighting in the Shenandoah Valley down below. "Stonewall" Jackson's Valley Campaign of 1862 was a masterpiece still studied by military men. Grandpa Traywick, my great-grandfather, fought in Jubal Early's

Valley Campaign of 1864 with a "Tar Heel" unit of North Carolinians until he was captured at Fisher's Hill. He was sent to Point Lookout, a Union Prisoner of War camp that had a higher mortality rate than the Confederate POW camp at Andersonville. He said the Yankees put them all into a long wagon train and galloped the teams all night down the Valley Pike to Winchester for fear of Mosby's Rangers. He wrote about his incarceration there in the *Southern Historical Society Papers*. Although Grandpa wasn't one of those who died there, his brother was, and he is buried there also. I remember my father telling me there was an old Confederate veteran living in his little hometown when he was growing up who said he had "*fit* all up and down the *She-NAN-do* Valley."

Except for General Jubal Early's desperate and ill-fated gamble at Cedar Creek against General Phil Sheridan — whose cavalry alone outnumbered Early's entire army — it all ended with "The Burning." Sheridan's troopers burned out the Valley clear and clean, burning barns and mills and smokehouses, taking horses and cattle and killing those they didn't want, destroying farm implements, the harvests, and all manner of provender on the edge of winter, until, as he told Grant, a crow flying over the Valley would have to carry his own rations. What the people there would have to do for rations to survive the coming winter, he did not say. Ah, but you should not have had the audacity to defy Lincoln's Government! The people of the Shenandoah — "Daughter of the Stars" — still smell the powder burning.

It is interesting to think that if a certain pebble were to drop into a certain place, it might lead to events that would change the course of a river. On the third day of July 1863, at Gettysburg, Lee's artillery expended much of its ammunition firing at the stone wall atop Cemetery Hill to "soften up" the Union position there for the great gamble of what has become known as "Pickett's Charge." But the cannon smoke obscured the target, and it was difficult for the gunners to see the effect they were having. As it turned out, their shots were high and were wreaking havoc among the wagon trains in the rear of the Union line. As a result, Pettigrew's Tar Heels failed to reach the wall, while Pickett's Virginians made it over but were obliterated. It was like just the tip of the spear penetrating the armor, but not quite deep enough to inflict a mortal wound.

There is a short story by Jack London entitled "A Piece of Steak." A boxer was to enter a championship fight that would provide for his hungry family if he won it or desperation if he lost, and he only wished for a piece of steak to give him the last bit of an edge that he would need. But the family had none to give him, so he had to do without. In the fight he landed the knockout punch that would have won the match for him, but his opponent got up at the count of nine and went on to win the championship. If only he had been able to have that piece of steak, that punch would have been hard enough to keep his opponent down for ten. The same as it was for Lee and Pickett on the third day at Gettysburg. If there had only been a piece of breeze to blow the smoke of the artillery fire away before the charge, the gunners could have seen their shots were a bit too high, they would have lowered the elevation on their guns just a wee bit, and there might now be three English-speaking countries in North America instead of two.

We did not gain the independence we deserved, but the struggle and the glory will forever be frozen in amber, while the victor is forever subjected to mortal corruption.

Just beyond Waynesboro I-64 merges with I-81, which runs southwestward into Tennessee. Waynesboro is where General Early fought his last skirmish. The remnants of his little army were scattered and Early and his staff barely escaped capture on Afton Mountain. General Early is buried in Spring Hill Cemetery on top of the hill that was his command post at the Battle of Lynchburg. Whenever I go there to visit my parents and my grandparents, I always go up the hill to salute "Old Jube."

I remember the cold winter day that Pastor Bill Burleigh gave the graveside eulogy for my mother. In her declining years I would frequently go to Lynchburg to spend time with her and we would go to hear Pastor Burleigh at Court Street Methodist Church, the church in which I was raised. The big old church on Court Street with its magnificent sanctuary and its pipe organ was always filled when I was growing up, but in later years when my mother and I would go, the choir outnumbered the congregation. General Lee's favorite hymn was "How Firm a Foundation," which is deeply moving. My father said my grandfather's favorite hymn was "In the Garden," and I remember singing it from the Methodist Hymnal at Court Street. But the one I like best, I think, is "Be Thou My Vision," sung to an old Irish melody, and I remember singing it, alone in the pew with my mother, in the beautiful, sad, empty old Court Street Methodist Church.

I-64 runs with I-81 for about twenty miles to Lexington before it breaks off and turns west again through the mountains towards Clifton Forge, Covington and the West Virginia line. Lexington is the home of the Virginia Military Institute and of Washington and Lee University, where General Lee was president after the war, and where he is buried in his Mausoleum under Valentine's famous sculpture, "The Recumbent Lee" in the Chancel of the Lee Chapel. It is a sepulcher worthy of King Arthur. Of course this has offended the sensibilities of today, so first all of the Battle Flags had to be removed, then a curtain had to be placed over the alcove, and finally a petition was installed to cover the Chancel altogether lest any hint of Lee's noble Christian character escape to taint any of the young scholars who may be near. But even that has not satisfied the administration, for now the headstone of Lee's charger Traveller has been removed from the horse's grave outside the chapel. As Admiral Raphael Semmes, CSN, observed, "Live asses will kick at dead lions."

In my day it was customary for VMI Cadets to render a salute when passing Lee Chapel on the way uptown. Winston Churchill said Lee was one of the noblest Americans who ever lived and one of the greatest captains in the annals of war, and Churchill was not alone in his estimation. When General Eisenhower was President, he had a picture of Lee in the Oval Office. As Thomas Carlyle said, it takes men of worth to recognize worth in men.

A lady once asked General Lee for his advice in the raising of her son. He simply said, "Teach him to deny himself." Such advice seems quaint today, when the Deep State elevates our every self-indulgence into a government "entitlement" in return for our vote, and then happily sells us and our children into slavery forever to a thirty trillion-dollar national debt to pay for it. We are discovering that slavery was not abolished after all; "Ole Marster" was merely exchanged for a Big Government demagogue and a Wall Street banker.

General Thomas J. "Stonewall" Jackson rests in Lexington as well, at what used to be named "Jackson Cemetery" until the town changed it so as not to offend anyone other than Southerners. Jackson lived here before the war serving as a Professor of Natural Philosophy at VMI, where the Cadets tormented him and called him "Tom Fool" Jackson for his many eccentricities — until they learned of his thunderbolt exploits in the war. His statue stood in front of barracks at Jackson Arch overlooking the parade ground for a hundred years, and the first year "Rats" at VMI had to salute his statue as they exited the arch. Flanked by the old Cadet Battery that had fought with the Cadets at the Battle of New Market, Jackson's statue personified the iron backbone of VMI. Gone, now, the one with the other. Jackson's statue has been removed, while his name has been sandblasted off of his arch and removed from Jackson Memorial Hall.

A hate filled and sanctimonious reporter for the Washington *Post*, taking the word of some Black ex-cadets who had been drummed out of VMI for lying, accused VMI of "systemic racism," and our groveling Governor at the time, once the President of the VMI Honor Court but now loving his office more than his honor, took them all at their word without question. He pronounced VMI guilty, fired the White Superintendent, hired a Black Superintendent, founded an office of Diversity, Equity, and Inclusion (DEI), and then launched a legal investigation against VMI to try and prove the charges were true. Governor Ralph Northam thus did more damage to VMI than did General David Hunter. In 1864, General Hunter only shelled and burned the Institute, whereas Governor Northam sold her soul for a mess of political pottage.

The Washington *Post* then insisted that VMI forget her Confederate heritage. At that time, I took out a full page ad in the Richmond *Times-Dispatch* that read as follows:

> "VMI's removal of any of her monuments for the sake of an ignoble appeasement is embracing a politically correct lie in violation of her Honor Code and a repudiation of her Cadets who died on the Field of Honor."

I remember marching in the Centennial New Market Day Parade on May 15, 1964. The band played "Dixie" and the Confederate Battle Flag was flying high at the head of the column as we marched by and saluted the graves of those ten Cadets killed at the Battle of New Market, and who rest there on Post under Sir Moses Ezekiel's statue of "Virginia Mourning Her Dead." So far the administration hasn't dug up those boys yet. Maybe they are just hoping nobody will notice. But the Battle Flags have been folded and put away now like some disreputable old uncle locked away in the attic, and the New Market Day Parade, a ceremony traditionally held every May 15th come rain, shine, earthquake or volcano on the most sacred day of the VMI calendar, has been relegated to some generic Memorial Day Parade on whatever day happens to be convenient.

But on a bluff five miles back up the Interstate from Lexington, a huge 30' x 30' Confederate Battle Flag flies high in the breeze for all to see.

There ain't no fergittin'...

*

II.

West Virginia

John Henry had a little woman,

Her name was Polly Ann.

John Henry got sick and he had to go to bed,

And Polly drove steel like a man, lord, lord.

Polly drove steel like a man.

A LITTLE BEYOND COVINGTON, Virginia, I-64 crosses the line into West Virginia at White Sulphur Springs. Until 1863, West Virginia was not in existence and was part of Virginia. This had given Virginia frontage along the Ohio River from above Wheeling, way up that little spike on the map that sticks up between Ohio and Pennsylvania just west of Pittsburg, all the way down to Huntington, in the western corner of the State made by West Virginia, Kentucky and Ohio. The Constitution says a State cannot be divided without that State's permission, and Virginia, busy fighting for her survival, did not give her permission, but Abraham Lincoln was a good political calculator and he could use some extra Electoral votes in the coming election of 1864. A man named Pierpont from up in Wheeling got himself anointed as the "Governor" of the "loyal State of Virginia" and some of his scalawag cronies got together as the "General Assembly." Establishing themselves in their "Capital" right across the river from Washington, and recognized by Lincoln as the "loyal" government of Virginia, they gave Lincoln "Constitutional permission" to divide

Virginia and West Virginia into two States. Virginia naturally objected — not that Virginia objected to secession, but quite the very opposite. She herself had not only seceded from the British Empire, she had voluntarily given up her Northwest Empire to the new Union after independence. She had then gladly agreed to Kentucky's desire to secede from Virginia in 1792, and she herself had seceded a second time, this time from the Union in 1861. But being ripped off by Lincoln's government and a cabal of scalawags was essentially just another matter of conquest as Lincoln took the United States across the line from a Jeffersonian Republic to a Hamiltonian Empire.

What at first glance seems ironic is that West Virginia was the last "slave State" to be admitted to the Union — six months after Lincoln's *Emancipation Proclamation*! But for those who have never read it, Lincoln's revered document plainly stated that slavery was just fine as long as one were loyal to his government. The United States continued to be a slave country throughout the war, and slaves there remained slaves until the ratification of the Thirteenth Amendment to the Constitution in December of 1865 after Lincoln and the Confederacy both were in their graves. Thus "Juneteenth" is a bogus holiday, but it is more fun to have festivals and cookouts in June than in December.

Emancipation not only freed the slave, it freed "Ole Marster" from having to take care of him from the cradle to the grave. Owning a slave doesn't give you free labor any more than owning a horse gives you a free ride. When Confederate Vice President Alexander Stephens asked Lincoln at the Hampton Roads Conference in 1865, what Lincoln proposed to do about taking care of the slaves he emancipated, Lincoln said "Let them root, hog, or die." So there's the freedom they got from the Yankees.

Jim Downs, in his book *Sick from Freedom*, relates how he had searched Freedman's Bureau documents and discovered that between 1862 and 1870 possibly as many as a million freed slaves, or one quarter of the population, died or became seriously ill under the care of their "liberators." That is more than the total number of soldiers who died, North and South combined, during the entire war. But during Reconstruction their votes were all that concerned their liberators. Their votes were needed in order to cement the carpetbaggers' plunder of the South, and the Party of Lincoln's control of the Central Government. Once those things had been accomplished the Blacks were then left free to "root, hog, or die" in the upheaval that had been wrought in the South, while the US Government, under Grant, Sherman, Sheridan and Custer, turned its attention to the Plains Indians who were in the way of the trans-continental railroads.

Between White Sulphur Springs and Lewisburg, Interstate 64 crosses the Greenbriar Valley. "Grandma Pearl," my great-grandmother, lived with her family on a farm there when she was a little girl. I was told that they could pick coal right from the sides of the hills. During the war the family "refugeed" back across the mountains to Liberty (now Bedford), Virginia, just west of Lynchburg at the foot of the Peaks of Otter. It was wintertime and there were few hotels for travelers as in our times, and it was customary for travelers to stop at farm houses along the way and ask for hospitality, which was always cordially granted to respectable people. It was a cold winter day and Grandma Pearl said her fingers had started to hurt as they all warmed themselves by the fire at the man's house. She said when she began to cry, the man gave her a shiny apple. After settling in Liberty she remembered awakening one night and creeping to the top of the stairs to hear her fifteen year old brother, home on leave from the army, sitting on the couch in the parlor with his mother, crying that he didn't want to go back, and his mother telling him that he had to go or he would be shot as a deserter.

The Greenbriar River runs southwesterly inside the West Virginia border to Hinton where it joins the New River. From there the New River runs northwesterly across the State as a tributary of the Kanawha River. The Kanawha runs past Charleston, the Capital of the State, and continues to the Ohio River. This had been the destination of the old James and Kanawha Canal, but how they intended to get a canal through those monstrous mountains is beyond me. I had studied Civil Engineering at VMI so I suppose it could have been done, for the railroads made it through with a great deal of tunneling using topographic maps, surveying equipment, steam drills, dynamite, mules, and convict labor.

Fifty miles into the State there is an exit off of the Interstate highway for Hinton, where the Greenbriar River makes a big bend before it joins the New River. Up the Greenbriar River a ways from Hinton, at the little community of Talcott, is the Big Bend Tunnel built by the Chesapeake & Ohio Railroad soon after the war. It was here that the legend of John Henry, "the steel driving man," was born. In my rambles a long time ago, I once met a man from Hinton who said he had known someone who had known John Henry. Scott Reynolds Nelson, one-time professor of history at William & Mary, did some research and wrote a book on the man. He said John Henry was a young Black man from New Jersey who had been convicted in a Virginia court for theft in 1866, and sentenced to ten years in the penitentiary. From there he was sent to work as convict labor with the C&O Railroad building tunnels on the line through West Virginia. Professor Nelson says John Henry worked on the Lewis Tunnel near Covington, Virginia, but the historical marker at the Big Bend Tunnel in West Virginia states that:

> "The great tunnel of the C&O Railroad was started at Big Bend in 1870 and completed three years later. It is more than a mile long, and now has a twin tunnel. Tradition makes this the scene of the steel drivers' ballad 'John Henry'."

The steel that was driven was a long steel drill bit used for drilling holes in rock for placing dynamite charges. One man, known as the "shaker," held the steel bit, rotating it a little after each blow, while the other man swung the hammer. The rock dust this created was inhaled into the lungs causing the early death of many men. Steam drills were used as well, but with water poured into the holes to keep down the deadly dust. It was dangerous work and there was always the very real danger of a tunnel collapse burying men, mules, and machines.

The Big Bend Tunnel is closed off now, with the newer alternate tunnel being used. But there is a monument to John Henry at the entrance to the old one, and stories have been told of the sound sometimes being heard of a hammer ringing on steel way back there in the tunnel. Who's to say not? For,

> *There are more things in Heaven and Earth, Horatio, than are dreamt of in your philosophy...*

The exit for Hinton off of the Interstate is at the New River Gorge. As dramatic as the gorge is there, further downstream near Fayetteville is the longest steel span in the Western Hemisphere and the third highest in the United States, carrying a US highway across the gorge. According to the National Park Service website, the bridge is listed in the National Register of Historic Places. In looking at the pictures one can only wonder how such a span of steel was constructed over such a gorge where no crane could ever be built to reach that high. The Park Service website explains how it was done: the steel was positioned over the gorge by trollies running on three inch diameter cables strung 3,500 feet between two sets of matching towers. Cor-ten steel, with a rust-like appearance that never needs painting, was used in the construction.

Building anything in West Virginia demands creative Civil Engineering solutions and the Interstate Highway system was no exception, for the roads span dizzying gorges, twist around towering mountains, and dip into hollers past small concentrations of houses deep in shadow for most of the daylight hours. The "big rigs" have to use the lower gears to make the climbs, and then stay in the lower gears coming down the other side on 7% grades for three miles or more. There are runaway truck ramps every mile or so. It is a hairy prospect and those drivers need to know what they are doing. I give them plenty of respect and plenty of room — and I most certainly don't want to have one breathing down my neck coming down off the mountain! I avoid trips out there during times of ice and snow, so I can only imagine what those truck drivers have to deal with in West Virginia when there is ice on the roads.

At Beckley, Interstate 64 merges with Interstate 77 and turns northward for Charleston fifty miles away. Before you get there you go through the toll booth for the West Virginia Turnpike. Luckily for me the Turnpike accepts the "EZ Pass" do-dad that I have stuck on the windshield of my car so I can breeze on through. The toll for cars is $4.25 entering and then another $4.25 coming off the turnpike as one breaks out of the big mountains coming into Charleston. Here the road runs along the Kanawha River, and one begins to see some industry, and occasionally a towboat bringing barges up the river.

Before I get into Charleston, I always take the Marmet/Chesapeake exit to fill up the car with gas and get some lunch. I have discovered a little hot dog stand there that serves hot dogs with chili and slaw. Hot dogs with chili and mustard and onions and sauerkraut and relish and all the other fixin's you can think of are not that hard to find, but hot dogs with chili and slaw on a steamed bun are a rare specialty these days. I remember as a boy growing up helping my father build fences on Saturdays. At lunchtime he would stop and say, "Come on, let's go down to the bottom and get a hot dog," and we would get in the car and go down to the C&S Café, a little hole-in-the-wall in Lynchburg on Hollins Mill Road by Blackwater Creek. I'd get two of the best hot dogs with chili and slaw on steamed buns that I have ever eaten in my life, and I'd wash them down with a freezing cold bottle of Dr. Pepper. Dad would tell me to slow down and not inhale them, but I would tell him that I couldn't wait to get my stomach around them. The C&S Café was a popular spot, but they only had about ten bar stools at the counter where you could sit and eat. Then one day they decided they were doing so well that they would expand. They enlarged the place and put in booths — and then no one came any more. But this little place in West Virginia had gotten a reputation, even from out of State. I would always stop there after picking up a cold beer at the convenience store next door and get two hot dogs with chili and slaw, and then find a shady spot in which to park the car while I sat and enjoyed the repast.

With lunch break over with, I found myself out of the mountains, zig-zagging my way back and forth across the Kanawha River and out of the Charleston Interstate exchanges. Somewhere in Charleston I found myself clear of the I-77 portion of the traffic and on the last leg of I-64 in West Virginia, with fifty miles to go to get to Huntington. Although the road opens up a bit after corkscrewing through the mountains, you are still hemmed in between river and hills for a ways before you break clear of both. But by then there is usually construction going on, lane shifts, concrete barriers and reduced speeds the rest of the way. Many people say they love the mountains, but the mountains always make me feel cramped up. I have always preferred the wide-open spaces and the empty places.

Huntington is an old town on the western end of West Virginia, and it is here that I get my first glimpses of the Ohio River. Commercial river traffic consisting of powerful towboats pushing rafts of barges loaded with coal or grain ply the Ohio through sets of locks as far up as Pittsburg, or they can go downriver to the Mississippi and all the way to New Orleans. The Interstate runs parallel to the river at Huntington for ten or fifteen miles and one can see it across the city from the Interstate in some places. History books tell us that Jesse James and his gang once robbed a bank here. It would seem they would have been a long way from home, but Frank and Jesse once had farms in Tennessee where they were living under aliases. In any case, at Huntington, West Virginia, I was getting my first exciting sense that I was approaching The West.

*

III.

Kentucky

Weep no more, my lady, oh, weep no more, today.
We sing one song for my old Kentucky home,
For my old Kentucky home far away.

SIX HOURS INTO MY TRIP I crossed the Big Sandy River into Kentucky at Ashland. Eastern Kentucky is on the Cumberland Plateau where the Kentucky coal fields are found. Coal mining was a staple industry here, as it was in West Virginia, but things change with the evolution of technology. Strip mining and big machines have replaced many of the rugged coal miners, economies based on coal suffer under the mania for "green energy," and an opioid epidemic has become a problem, just as it has been in southwestern Virginia with tobacco going out and textile mills and furniture factories going overseas to China and other places where cheap labor is plentiful. The result for the people of the mountains — some whose families have been here since before the Revolutionary War — is a struggle with poverty and hard times. One can hear it in the heartfelt songs that come from these Kentucky coal fields sung by such artists as Loretta Lynn and *Coal Miner's Daughter*, or Patty Loveless and *You'll Never Leave Harlan Alive*, or Billy Ed Wheeler and his *Coal Tattoo*:

I stood for the union, walked in the line,

Fought against the company.

I stood for the U. M. W. of A.

Now who's gonna stand for me?

I got no home and I got no pay,

Just got a worried soul:

And this blue tattoo on the side of my head

Left by the number nine coal.

    According to the National Park Service website, the first European settlers on the rugged Cumberland Plateau were of predominantly English and Scotch-Irish ancestry coming from Virginia and North Carolina in the late 1700s. They established small, isolated farms along the creeks and river bottoms and established self-sufficient communities where industry was limited to water-powered grist mills, moonshining, and niter mining for the making of gunpowder. Guerilla warfare in the War Between the States further isolated the region. The Daniel Boone National Forest, which Interstate 64 crosses, covers much of this rugged region.

    Coming down off of the Cumberland Plateau into the Bluegrass Region is the old town of Mt. Sterling, home of the 220-year-old October Court Day. According to the tourist board, Mt. Sterling had been an early trading center for Eastern Kentucky, with hotels and taverns serving as meeting places and stagecoach stops. After Kentucky had become a State in 1792, the General Assembly decided that each county should meet once a month for holding court. October Court Day held here became an annual trading day and it has been carried on down through the years. Today people come from miles around to this four-day event to buy, sell and trade antiques, tools, crafts, artwork and collectibles, and to enjoy the local cuisine.

Just beyond Mt. Sterling is Winchester, which is the headquarters of the Boone National Forest. Upon my graduation from VMI, I took a job that was offered to me here by the Forest Service as a GS-5 Civil Engineer. They had offered me this job with the full knowledge that I would soon be taking a commission in the US Army. My office was at Winchester and I remember serving in that capacity for two weeks before going into the military. Upon my return from Vietnam, I resigned my commission at the completion of my obligation and was offered my position again with the Forest Service — with seniority! But by that time I was on a "quest for the Truth" and I graciously declined the offer.

The Daniel Boone National Forest is named, of course, for the legendary frontiersman who became famous for his exploration and settlement of Kentucky. He was born in 1734 in Pennsylvania before his family moved to North Carolina. In 1769 he led the expedition that blazed the trail through the Cumberland Gap — located at the far western tip of Virginia — that was followed by the early pioneers into Kentucky. Daniel Boone established a fort — named Boonesborough — near what is now Richmond, Kentucky, where he became leader, and where he brought his family to settle. He struggled with the Indians, rescuing his daughter from captivity at one point and later escaping from captivity himself at another. But events developed against him at Boonesborough, and he, a consummate frontiersman to the last, moved west to Missouri, where he died of natural causes in 1820 at the ripe old age of 85.

Winchester is also the birthplace of the poet Allen Tate, one of the twelve "Vanderbilt Fugitives" who wrote essays for the 1930s classic Southern Manifesto *I'll Take My Stand: The South and the Agrarian Tradition*. In the Introduction to the 1962 Torchbook Edition, Louis D. Rubin, Jr., wrote that "It was the vision of poets, and carried with it certain convictions about living and dying that have held much imaginative appeal to Southerners and many non-Southerners as well. This, I think, is the essential function of *I'll Take My Stand*, and accounts for the book's continuing hold on the

Southern imagination. It is a rebuke to materialism, a corrective to the worship of Progress, and a reaffirmation of man's aesthetic and spiritual needs." As Allen Tate wrote of crossing the line from the agrarian life into the industrial age:

> *Lean to the crowded air and hear,*
>
> *Eavesdropper, how it goes inside*
>
> *Your own deaf and roaring ear:*
>
> *Boys caress the machines they ride*
>
> *On the Day of Jubilo.*

In the lobby of a rest stop along the Interstate in the Bluegrass section of the State, posted over the board containing maps and brochures for tourists, it says "Kentucky is the Front Porch of the South." Before the war, Harriet Beecher Stowe came down from New England to Kentucky and visited there for two weeks. With that as her authority on slavery in the South she went back home and wrote *Uncle Tom's Cabin*, setting hair on fire in the North for its lurid depictions and in the South for its lurid lies. When the war broke out Kentucky refused to send troops to Lincoln. She tried to remain neutral, but Abraham Lincoln was desperate to keep her in the Union. By early 1862 Union troops controlled most of the State, and in 1863, when Lincoln issued his *Emancipation Proclamation*, it did not apply to Kentucky.

Kentucky's neutrality failed and a Confederate "shadow government" was formed. Kentucky was admitted to the Confederacy on December 10, 1861, and was given the thirteenth star in the Confederate Flag. Although Kentucky ended up giving more troops to the North (mostly infantry), she provided valuable troops to the South as well (mostly cavalry). Generals John C. Breckinridge and Simon Bolivar Buckner were Kentuckians, and General John Hunt Morgan with his Kentucky cavalry crossed the Ohio and raided southern Indiana and Ohio, sending shockwaves through the region:

Morgan, Morgan the Raider,

And Morgan's terrible men,

With Bowie knives and pistols

Galloping up the glen...

General Basil Duke, who had been second in command under Morgan, escorted Jefferson Davis (who had been born in Kentucky) and the Confederate Government southward with his Kentucky Cavalry at the fall of Richmond. After the war, Kentucky elected so many Confederate veterans to office that it was said that Kentucky didn't really secede until after Appomattox.

Twenty miles or so west of Winchester is Lexington, "The Horse Capital of the World." It is in the heart of the Bluegrass Region, which is noted for its thoroughbred horse farms and racetracks. The Kentucky Horse Park, the International Museum of the Horse, and the Keeneland Race Track are here, and Thoroughbred sales are held here every fall of the year.

Lexington was also the home of Senator Henry Clay (1777-1852). Clay was born in Hanover County, Virginia, and came to be a Kentucky statesman, representing her at one time or another in both the House and the Senate. He was one of the "Great Triumvirate" of Clay, Webster, and Calhoun. He sponsored the "American System," which was rooted in the centralizing plans of Alexander Hamilton, and included high tariffs, a central bank and a national system of internal improvements. This was objected to by the South for its leading to crony capitalism and an unconstitutionally powerful central government. Clay served as Secretary of State under the New Englander John Quincy Adams from 1825 to 1829. In the Senate, John Randolph of Roanoke (that is, *Roanoke*, his plantation in Charlotte County, Virginia), a staunch States Rights Constitutionalist, described the contested arrangement by which Adams became President and Clay his Secretary of State as a deal between "the Puritan (Adams) and the blackleg (Clay)." Clay challenged Randolph to a duel which Randolph accepted, stating that he had no intention of killing Clay. They met across the river from

Washington on Virginia soil. Both missed on the first shot. Clay put a hole in Randolph's coat with his second, whereupon Randolph shot his pistol into the air. He then went over and said, "You owe me a coat, Mr. Clay," and they both shook hands. But in his subsequent political career John Randolph said he wanted to be buried facing west so he could keep an eye on Henry Clay.

Not far past Lexington is Frankfort, the Capital of the State. Along the way and beyond towards Louisville one passes several exits that take you to advertised whisky distilleries, another thing for which Kentucky is noted. I have no time for that because this first day on the road will be a long one, and by this time in my trip I am usually going to find myself in the middle of Louisville's five o'clock rush hour traffic.

One of my concessions to the conveniences of modern times is the use of the amazing GPS on my cell phone. I usually just plug in my destination for that day at the outset and let the nice AI lady tell me about road closures, speed traps and traffic jams up ahead. Often in times of rush hour traffic, she will take me off of the normally direct route and lead me around a bypass. She is a very pleasant lady and she lets me know that "this is your fastest route," even if the traffic is thick. How she knows that is beyond me. However, she can be a nag sometimes when I take an exit to a service station or a restaurant, at which time she keeps telling me to go this way and that or around Robin Hood's barn to get back on the highway. Sometimes her voice even pesters me from my pocket while I am trying to eat at a restaurant.

Louisville ("LOOuh-vll" as we are supposed to say in almost two syllables instead of three) is home to the Kentucky Derby. To think of all the money and the breeding and the training and the doctoring and the calculations that go into a horse race, and then to watch the horses nobly run their hearts out without guile, can be enough to break your own. Louisville is also a river port with a number of big bridges spanning the Ohio River. Old-fashioned-looking diesel-powered "steamboats" are tied up alongside the levee for taking tourists on tours. I can't watch the river while I am crossing the bridge in heavy traffic, but occasionally I glimpse a mighty towboat pushing a raft of loaded barges upriver against the current, seeming to be almost standing still.

Then I am across the Ohio River and into Indiana.

*

IV.

INDIANA

All up and down the whole Creation,

Sadly I roam —

Still longing for the old plantation,

And for the old folks at home.

IF IT WERE WINTER, IT WOULD BE getting dark by now, but it is late spring and I am still chasing the sun to Evansville, Indiana — my destination for the night. I have nearly two more hours to go. Interstate 64 runs along the southern border of Indiana roughly parallel to the Ohio River. The country in the eastern part of the State there is wooded with rolling hills and the road runs through occasional cuts in stratified rock, much like I had found in Kentucky. There are rare chances to find a filling station, so I try to make sure ahead of time that my car has enough gas to get me to Evansville.

In my trips back and forth to Kansas I try to make the first day the long day. Going out, I figure three hours in Virginia, three hours in West Virginia, three hours in Kentucky, and then two hours across Indiana to Evansville, which is another river port on the Ohio. Counting stops for hot dogs and gas it makes for a solid twelve-hour day on the road. I don't stay in Evansville proper but at the intersection of I-64 and US 41 about ten miles or so north of town. It is out in the flat farmlands of western Indiana that my grandfather had described to me long ago. There are several truck stops, fast food joints, and four or five motels/hotels very conveniently located near that intersection. I have stayed at several and found them all to be just fine — not the Royal Palms Hilton, but clean, friendly, basic accommodations that serve contractors, long-haul truckers, and people like me very well. By the time I get there, fuel up the car and check in, I am ready to have a beer and a hamburger and then lay my weary head down for the night. No wonder the long-haul truckers, "sailors on a concrete sea," have to keep a log book with their hours — and the police do check them. All along the Interstate, on the shoulders of exit ramps, at truck stops and at rest areas, you will see the big rigs parked when the driver has made his limit of hours for the day and is "sacked out" back there in the sleeper cab of his truck. Sometimes along the way I pass a black and orange Schneider truck, and for half of a split second I think my son Rob might be driving that rig — but then, no....

The next morning I am up early. I fill my tall "go cup" with coffee (and maybe sometimes a little splash of Jack Daniels for a sweetener) and I am on the road again, making good time before 6 o'clock in the morning. Evansville is just the other side of the time zone so I am now on Central Standard Time. My father, who traveled for a living, always said early morning was the best time of day and I am inclined to agree with him. With the sun just barely coming up through the trees behind me and yet to be burning the mist off of the broad fields and flatlands, the morning is mild and I have the windows rolled down thinking what a blessing it is to be alive.

It was on this last twenty-five mile stretch before I got to Illinois, and on this glorious morning, that I got to thinking about my grandfather who was from out here in the flat farmlands of Indiana, and how I ought to write about him and about my travels out this way.

Pop and Nanny were my maternal grandparents and they both had grown up on farms in the Midwest — Pop in Indiana and Nanny in Iowa. They lived next door to us in Virginia when I was growing up. Their house was of brick with a screened-in side porch on one end where they would sleep on roll-a-way beds at night in the hot summertime, with the lightening bugs winking in the tall oaks on the broad lawn in front of the house. They would have a fan going, of course, because these were in the prehistoric days before air conditioning. They also had a black-and-white television set out there so they could watch the Lawrence Welk Show. Pop would always put up awnings around the porch in the summer to keep the rain from blowing in.

When my grandparents were first married they lived in Chicago, where my Uncle Dick was born in 1914. Pop volunteered to serve in the First World War, but they wouldn't take him because he had a family. At some point Pop was given two job offers to teach — one in Virginia and one somewhere else. My grandmother — "a Virginian stopping over in the Midwest for a few generations" — said, "Oh, we must go to Virginia!" for she had Virginia blood that went way back, maybe even to Pocahontas, for her grandmother was a Bolling. (My mother always claimed that kin.) There was also some ancestor who had settled on Lamb's Creek in the Northern Neck of Virginia, and another who was an officer in the militia that had stormed Kings Mountain during the Revolution.

Nanny's grandfather was also a Virginian. He had been born in 1828, and had ridden west out of Virginia on a mare named "Little Nell." He became a Plainsman, running freight wagon trains across the High Plains to Fort Denver when Denver was nothing but an Army fort. He once had been given the opportunity to buy a parcel of land there, but he turned it down. That parcel later turned out to be in the middle of downtown Denver, Colorado. One morning a young stranger road into their wagon camp and was invited to breakfast. In the old Code of the West, you didn't ask too many questions of strangers. Later in the day a posse came through looking for Billy the Kid — but of course no one had seen anyone. At one point a young man named William F. Cody had been his scout. Many years later, when Pop was courting Nanny in Iowa, the family went to see "Buffalo Bill" Cody's Wild West Show. Grandpa Crisman, the old Plainsman, was standing with them watching the parade when Buffalo Bill came prancing by on his horse, tipping his hat and bowing to the crowd left and right. He spied my great-great-grandfather and said, "Well I'll be! It's Johnny Crisman!" and he hopped off of his horse and came over and shook his hand. We have a photo of Grandpa Crisman among the family treasures. It shows a white-haired old man in shirtsleeves standing ramrod-straight and tough as whip leather. Nanny told me he didn't talk much, but she knew he had killed men. The rocking chair he had made with his own hands is still in the family.

So Nanny and Pop moved to Virginia, but Nanny always loved the Midwest, too. One day I asked her, "Nanny, how come you say 'WAHter' instead of 'WARter'"? She said, "That's the way they say water in Iowa, but I'll make a deal with you; if you will say 'cow' instead of 'cyow,' then I'll say 'warter.'" A little later I came back and said, "Nanny, I can't do it. You can go ahead and say 'wahter.'"

Nanny was an avid reader and I remarked on it even at my early age. She liked to read historical novels by good writers about Virginia and Carolina. Some of her books that I remember were Ellen Glasgow's *The Battle-Ground* and *Vein of Iron*, and Inglis Fletcher's series of books, such as *The Scotswoman, Bennett's Welcome, Men of Albemarle, Roanoke Hundred*, and *Lusty Wind for Carolina*. She left me a wonderful legacy in that regard. Nanny was also a wonderful cook, noted for her potato salad, fried chicken and biscuits. "Take two and butter them while they are hot," she would say. Put chicken gravy on them, too, and know Heaven on earth. In the summertime we would load up with summer vegetables from the garden down in the back. In the fall and winter we would go one year to her house for Thanksgiving dinner and to my paternal grandparent's house in South Carolina for Christmas. Then the next year we would switch the visits around.

My mother and my Aunt Betty were both born in Lynchburg. When my parents were married after my father returned home from the war in Burma, they were living at Ft. Benning, Georgia — or whatever Politically Correct name they have changed it to now. But when I was expected to make my grand debut into this world my mother returned to Lynchburg so that I would be born on Virginia soil. About the time that I was three my father built a house on a gravel road that soon became a wonderful paved road neighborhood full of boys my age. My grandparents built a house next door and my Uncle Dick built a house on the other side of them. Aunt Betty was married to a career Naval officer, but she and my cousins Michele and Mary would often stay with Nanny and Pop when Uncle Ed was at sea.

Pop was a storyteller and from my earliest days I loved to hear him tell stories about his brother Medford and him growing up on the farm in Indiana. When they were boys, they evidently were much like Laurel & Hardy — with Uncle Medford as always the fall guy. Pop told me that Medford was "not the practical one" in the family, but he ended up as an accomplished artist and he at one time ran a successful cartoon strip in the Chicago *Tribune*.

Pop's grandfather was from Germany (my mother told me from the Salzburg Valley, I think, but I can't ask her now). With the coming of the Industrial Revolution in the middle of the nineteenth century, Europe, from Italy to England, was in a Socialist turmoil and many Europeans migrated to the United States. During the War Between the States, many Germans with no better prospects were met by recruiting sergeants on the docks of Philadelphia and New York and offered lucrative bounties to join Lincoln's Armies. I don't know when my great-great grandfather arrived, but I never heard that he was ever a mercenary in the Union Army. Nor was he the type to be involved with the revolutions of the Socialists, who were so busy saving the world that they did not have time to provide for their families, for he walked from Pennsylvania to Indiana beside a wagon and a team of oxen and cleared sixty acres with an ax when he got there.

His son — Pop's father — was known to be an excellent farmer, but he elected to manage the farms of others for the steady security it offered rather than to have one of his own. Frontier entertainment on Sunday afternoons would consist of contests of strength. Two men would face off, each with one hand gripped on the back of the other man's belt and the other gripped to the back of his collar. The object was to see who could drive the other man's head into the dirt. This was before the days of video games. Pop's father evidently fared well in those contests for he was strong enough to put his back between the front legs of a horse and lift him off the ground to put shoes on his hooves. That might have just been for show, however, for Dolly

Saddler, our old Black farrier, would merely lift a hoof between his knees to trim and file it and nail on the shoe the way all farriers do that I know of. Pop's father once saw a man whipping his horse and he went over and gave the man a thrashing. Our great-grandfather's blood still runs strongly in my Cousin Mary's veins. That, mixed with her father's pure Fighting Irish blood, makes for a daunting combination for anyone to face if she ever catches them mistreating a dog.

Pop's father was managing a farm in Indiana when it was suggested that he homestead in North Dakota and have a farm of his own. They loaded up a covered wagon and gave it a try, but the winter weather was so brutal in the northern High Plains that they didn't stay. My grandfather said that the land was so flat and treeless and devoid of landmarks that at the end of a day of plowing he would have to rely on the horse to find his way back home. One day while plowing alone way out on the plains, he was astonished to hear beautiful strains of Celestial Music passing over his head. He said he knew he wasn't imagining it because the horse stopped and perked up his ears to listen to it, too.

Although the family moved back to Indiana, Pop would hop freights to North Dakota to help with the wheat harvest. Once in the Chicago yards he saw a boy try to grab the door of a moving boxcar and lose his grip. The boy swung under the wheels and got both legs cut off. In giving me tips for a future career, Pop told me to always grab the forward ladder of a moving car. That way if you miss the stirrup you will be swung into the side of the car and knocked away, whereas if you miss the stirrup on the ladder at the rear of the car you will be swung between the cars and under the wheels. I didn't try it at the time, but down in the woods from our house by Blackwater Creek ran the tracks of the Norfolk and Western Railroad. The N&W hauled a lot of coal, and back then they still ran the old steam engines. Lying in bed at night with the windows open in the summertime I could hear that lonesome old steam whistle blow for a hundred miles.

Hearing all of his wonderful stories about growing up on the farm, I asked Pop why he didn't stay. He said the work was always hard and he couldn't wait to get away at the first opportunity. He was a scholar and an athlete with a sharp mind and an athletic body. He boxed, was a gymnast, and ran the hundred-yard dash, and I think on the day before he died he could still outrun me across the front yard! He earned a Law Degree but he said the study of law was so dry that he didn't like it, so he studied business and became a teacher and then an accountant. I asked him why he liked accounting and he said he liked to do "figgers." He did not become a CPA because he said he liked to solicit his own business. He would not take accounts with places that sold alcohol, but he had accounts all around Southside in towns such as Altavista, Halifax and South Boston as well as in Lynchburg. Whenever he would leave for business he always had on a suit and tie and a fresh white shirt, and he wore one of those hats that men wore back in the 'forties and 'fifties with the brim turned down in the front and turned up in the back. He drove a LaSalle and he was very proud of his driving, sitting up straight like he was driving a fine carriage. One day he had some checks and receipts in the back seat of the car and my little cousin Mary and I, being *very* naughty, got in and tore them up for no reason except for badness. We both richly deserved a good switching, but afterwards, when Pop found out about it, we heard that he had patiently sorted through the mess, taped everything all back together and never said a word about it. "Don't be too hard on the children," he would say, "You don't want to break their spirit." Nonetheless, at my house we had a flourishing switch bush conveniently located by the back porch, but I digress....

Pop and Nanny had a big garden down in the back yard with everything you could think of in it — corn, tomatoes, cucumbers, string beans, butter beans, squash, pumpkins and watermelons. Inspired by his farm stories and wishing I was on a farm myself, I would go and help them tend it. One summer day he took me down there and we pulled up some radishes, took them back to the house, washed them off, and snipped off the roots. He then got a coffee saucer and poured some salt into it, and we sat together at the kitchen table munching on radishes dipped in salt.

Another time, in the shade on the back terrace, he taught me how to sharpen a pocketknife on a whetstone. He also taught me how to sharpen a pencil, for a pencil and an old-timey adding machine with that roll of paper were his stock in trade, and he could sharpen a pencil with his pocketknife better than those hand-crank sharpeners we had at school. He also taught me the proper way to hold a pencil when I wrote. English cursive is written from left to right, of course, so for right-handed people the letters come into view out from under their hand as they write. For left-handed people, though, it is just the opposite and the words are covered. This explains why left-handed people sometimes try to write with their hand all cramped around. I happen to be left-handed, but Pop told me to write with the eraser-end of the pencil pointed towards the shoulder of my writing hand. I have done so all of my life ever since and it works just fine. But in today's digital age I understand they don't even teach cursive writing in school anymore. Then how, may I ask, are our children supposed to go up in the attic and read the treasured letters stored there that their grandfather wrote to their grandmother?

Driving along with the windows rolled down on that beautiful soft morning through the flat farmlands of Indiana that my grandfather had described to me so long ago, drinking coffee with the early morning sun coming up behind me not yet burning the mist off of the fields, I felt it was a blessing from God to be alive on that morning, and my thoughts went back to those stories that Pop had told me and the things that he had taught me. I was becoming aware that these trips to Kansas had become more than just spatial, and that the fourth dimension had become more than just time logged on the highway. In following the Interstate highway from Virginia to Kansas I was also following the spatial and temporal line of America's birth, growing pains and westward migrations — and towards what sunset, I wondered? In thinking of these things, it occurred to me that I had been only one handshake away from the days of the pioneers, for Pop said in his lifetime he had walked alongside of a covered wagon and he had lived to see the flights of jet airplanes across the skies. He died the year man first set foot on the moon.

So here's to you, Pop! You were a wonderful grandfather, and I miss you.

*

V.

Illinois

Listen to the jingle, the rumble, and the roar

As she glides along the woodlands,

Through the hills and by the shore.

Hear the mighty rush of the engine,

Hear the lonesome hobo squall

While traveling through the jungle

On the Wabash Cannonball.

THE WABASH RIVER is the boundary line between Indiana and Illinois, and I crossed it early in the morning with *The Wabash Cannonball* running through my head. A little research on the internet (another of my concessions to modernity I must confess) reveals that the Wabash Cannonball was a daytime passenger express service between Detroit and St. Louis that ran through Illinois on the Wabash Railroad from 1950 to 1971. It was discontinued with the formation of Amtrak, but there is a Wabash Cannonball Bridge that spans the Wabash River maybe fifty miles upstream from the I-64 crossing. Some say the train was named after a hobo folk song from the nineteenth century about a mythical train that was cursed to run the rails forever, and that a hobo would only see it when the train came to take him to his rewards. Such ghost stories about trains brings to mind that of the West Point Light seen occasionally along the railroad down at West Point, Virginia, on the Pamunky River. Some say it is the ghost of a brakeman whose head had been cut off on the railroad and he is walking the tracks at night with a lantern searching for it, while others say it is just marsh gas that is so light that it follows you when you try to walk away from it. Take your pick.

Illinois, like Indiana, Ohio, Michigan and Wisconsin, was part of the Old Northwest Territory that Virginia relinquished to the new Union after the Revolutionary War. The history of the region may be readily found by searching the internet. Before the Revolution, Britain had issued the Proclamation of 1763 which prohibited White colonial settlement west of the Appalachian Mountains. This angered the colonists and became a factor leading to the Revolutionary War. During the war in 1779, George Rogers Clark of the Virginia Militia captured Kaskaskia (which is in Illinois on the Mississippi River) and Vincennes (which is in Indiana on the Wabash River) from the British. Virginia then laid claim to the whole Old Northwest and called it Illinois County. Britain officially ceded the territory to the United States with the Treaty of Paris in 1783 and Virginia ceded her claims to the territory north of the Ohio River to the new Union in 1784, earning her the sobriquet "The Mother of States."

Thomas Jefferson organized the territory with the Land Ordinance of 1784, which provided for it to be divided into States. The Land Ordinance of 1785 made provisions for surveying the land and dividing it into parcels for sale and settlement. The Northwest Ordinance of 1787, based on earlier recommendations of Thomas Jefferson, provided for the formation of no fewer than three and no more than five States which would be admissible to the Union when the number of free inhabitants reached 60,000. Slavery and involuntary servitude were to be prohibited — a legal clause that would prove to be the foundation of much contention in the Western Territories in the future. Settlement followed the forts, and forts that were no longer garrisoned were an indication that the Indians were no longer a threat in the area. Ohio was granted Statehood in 1803. By 1813, when Tecumseh was defeated and killed, the frontier had essentially been moved west to the Mississippi. Indiana became a State in 1816 and Illinois in 1818.

States formed from the territories were to pass some of the earliest and most stringent "Jim Crow" Laws in the United States. Not only had slavery been prohibited within their bounds, but these laws prohibited free Blacks from residing within their bounds as well. John Randolph of Roanoke freed his slaves in his will and had purchased a large tract of land for them to settle on in Ohio, but when they left Virginia to claim their bequest the citizens of Ohio ran them off and stole their land. The "Underground Railroad" ran through Illinois all the way up to Canada because the Black "passengers" were not allowed to "disembark" in "The Land of Lincoln."

Illinois is "The Land of Lincoln" and it is lavishly proclaimed on the license plates and elsewhere. Abraham Lincoln, of course, was the sixteenth President of the United States and President during the War Between the States. He is the most deified politician since Julius Caesar, worshipped in his Olympian Temple on the Washington Mall for "Freeing the Slaves and Saving the Union."

The Lincoln Myth is fiercely guarded by Ivy League "Gatekeepers," for it is fragile and crumbles under close examination. Legend has it that he was born in a log cabin in Kentucky in 1809 to Thomas Lincoln and Nancy Hanks, but Howard Ray White, co-founder of the Society of Independent Southern Historians, claims otherwise in his extensively researched book entitled *Rebirthing Lincoln, A Biography: How an Illinois Lawyer Kept Secret His Illegitimate Birth and Won the 1860 Presidential Nomination of the Northern States Republican Party.* White gives convincing evidence that Lincoln was sired by Abraham Enloe, a well-to-do North Carolinian living in the Smoky Mountains, when Nancy Hanks was employed in his household as a maid, and that Lincoln was not born in 1809, but four years earlier and named Abraham after his natural father. All of his life Lincoln went to extraordinary lengths to conceal his illegitimate birth, the news of which in those days would have destroyed his political career. White does not have a picture of Abraham Enloe in his book but he has one of

Lincoln's half-brother, Wesley Enloe, posted alongside of a picture of Lincoln before he had a beard. Both are extraordinarily tall, lanky, and rawboned men like their father, and side-by-side they could almost be the "spittin' image" of one another. On the other hand, Thomas Lincoln, who history claims to be his father, was a man of an ordinary height and build that is nowhere near that of Abraham Lincoln's. As John Randolph of Roanoke said of the fine horses he was noted for raising, "the blood will tell in a four-mile heat."

Abraham Enloe, who was a married man, felt a responsibility for Nancy Hanks and her son and he took them to Kentucky to live with the family of Nancy's mother. While there he was introduced to Thomas Lincoln, who took a kindly interest in Nancy Hanks and her little boy. Enloe eventually persuaded Thomas Lincoln to marry Nancy Hanks and take care of her son, and he gave Lincoln five hundred dollars (a tidy sum in those days) when he agreed. Young Abraham was then given the name Lincoln.

In 1816, Thomas Lincoln sold his land in Kentucky and took the family to southern Indiana where he staked a claim. On Interstate 64 there are signs pointing to "Abraham Lincoln's Boyhood Home." In 1818, Nancy Hanks died. The following year Thomas Lincoln married Sarah Bush Johnston. Both she and Nancy Hanks were good mothers to young Abe, but in later years Lincoln rarely mentioned either of them.

In 1830, Thomas Lincoln sold his land in Indiana and moved to Illinois. Before leaving Indiana, Abraham Lincoln had developed an interest in politics, and in Illinois he became a Whig. He was a devoted follower of Henry Clay and his "American System," which advocated a strong central government, national improvements with high tariffs to fund them, and a national bank. In 1842, Lincoln married Mary Todd, of Lexington, Kentucky, after a long courtship when she was visiting some of her family in Illinois. By then Lincoln had become a successful lawyer and a railroad lobbyist heavily involved in politics. When Thomas Lincoln died in 1851, Lincoln did not attend the funeral, claiming he was too busy with his law practice. For twenty years he had studiously avoided contact with Thomas and Sarah Lincoln for fear that the truth of his illegitimate birth would be exposed. "Honest Abe" had even gone so far as to create a false record of his birth. Two years after Thomas Lincoln's death, Abraham Lincoln purchased a Bible and surprised his long-ignored stepmother, Sarah, with a visit. While there he recorded — in his own hand — all of the family birth dates in the newly purchased Bible, and he listed his own as "February 12th 1809, son of Thomas and Nancy Lincoln."

Lincoln gained national political prominence debating Democrat Stephen Douglas, the "Little Giant," in a series of debates in 1858. In 1860, Lincoln, now a prominent lawyer for the railroads, became the presidential candidate for the Republican Party, the new political party of the North's mercantile interests. The Republicans, using the Machiavellian tactics of "divide and rule," split the Democrat Party of the agrarian South and the agrarian West over the issue of slavery in the Territories and won the election of 1860, prompting the secession of seven States of the Deep South. Cotton was "King" at that time, and with the "Cotton Kingdom" out of the Union and free trading with Europe, the North's nascent "Mercantile Kingdom" — resting heavily on the manufacture and shipment of Southern cotton and the tariffs that Southern imports brought to it — would collapse. Lincoln determined to drive the "Cotton Kingdom" back into the Union, so he brushed off Southern diplomats wishing to negotiate a peaceful separation and launched an armada against Charleston Harbor to provoke the South into firing the first shot. South Carolina responded to Lincoln's provocation just as Massachusetts, "The Patriot State," had responded to King George's provocation at Lexington and Concord in 1775, and Lincoln got the war he wanted.

Lincoln was no abolitionist. He was a political animal with a wet digit continually stuck in the air to see which way the political wind was blowing. During the Lincoln — Douglas debates of 1858 he made it plain that he had no intention of introducing political and social equality between the White and Black races. At his Inauguration in 1861, Lincoln said he had no intention of interfering with slavery where it already existed, but that he was only waging war to "save the Union" and to "collect the revenue."

Radical Abolitionists in the North were small in numbers but large in noise, and they were considered to be mostly busybody nuisances. The numbers of altruistic Radical Abolitionists were to be found in inverse proportion to their distance away from the South and from the practical problems of emancipation — which were something akin to trying to mix oil and water. The further one gets from an issue, either in time or space, the more abstract the issue becomes, and the easier it is for one to post one's virtues by dealing with it strictly on the basis of morality. New England Abolitionists had their pet Negroes like Frederick Douglass whom they could show off and fawn over, but the thought of their White Puritan stronghold being overrun by a horde of Black Africans, such as in South Carolina or Mississippi, would have horrified them.

The Radical Abolitionists in Lincoln's cabinet, however, were less altruistic and more calculating. They had long-term political plans of power laid out for themselves that depended first upon emancipation, so it was to their advantage for the war to go on long enough until emancipation became a war issue. Halfway through the war, when the South was on the verge of winning her independence, the time was ripe for them to force Lincoln to issue his limited *Emancipation Proclamation*. This proclamation would provide several advantages to the North's war effort. *First*, it would keep Europe from recognizing the Confederacy and breaking the North's naval blockade of the South, *Second*, it would disrupt the Confederacy's "support troops" by causing slaves to run away, and *Third*, if they were lucky, it might even inaugurate a slave insurrection that would empty the Confederate ranks as men rushed home to defend their families from slaughter. However, they were to be disappointed in this last.

This emancipation plan was devised by the Radical Republicans as a purely political consideration and not for any altruistic reasons, because the war was not waged for the slave (as "The Myth of American History" would have it), but against his master. The Republicans wanted his cotton, which is why they wouldn't let him leave the Union, but they didn't want his politics, for the Southern planter was the political stumbling block that had been preventing the North from creating a powerful central government ever since the days of Alexander Hamilton. So the ultimate plan of these Radicals was *First*: to use the war to emancipate the slaves in the South and destroy the Southern planter and his politics (they could still get impoverished sharecroppers to raise all the cotton they wanted after the war); *Second*: after the war, to disenfranchise the White people of the South and to enfranchise the freed slaves; *Third*: to teach them to hate "Ole Marster" and to vote for the carpetbaggers; and *Fourth*: to use them as political tools to make the Southern States Republican in order to cement the Republican Party's control of the country. There was only one problem: when the war ended, Lincoln's plan was to "let the South up easy." That would throw a big monkey-wrench into all of their carefully calculated plans for political power. But no worries there, for John Wilkes Booth assassinated Abraham Lincoln right on time and took care of that problem.

Lincoln had become hated and reviled in the North when the "butcher's bill" for his war had come due. To protect his political position from his opponents he had arbitrarily suspended the writ of *habeas corpus*, destroyed opposition printing presses to silence the media, and threw tens of thousands of his political opponents into prison without trial. Everyone else was intimidated into silence. But when Lincoln was assassinated, the Radicals took it as a Heaven-sent blessing, elevated "Father Abraham, the Great Emancipator" to martyrdom, claimed Jefferson Davis was complicit in his murder, and stoked the North's white-hot rage against the South during the vindictive "Reconstruction."

I once asked my paternal grandmother, who had been born and raised on a plantation in Buckingham County, Virginia, twenty years after the war, what she thought of Lincoln. She said he was the only friend the South had after Appomattox. When I asked my mother, she said with friends like that who needs enemies? My fourth-grade teacher was a Yankee who was as crabby as a sour apple. She took revenge on us for having to teach Virginia history by making us memorize Lincoln's *Gettysburg Address* — his classic example of Orwelllian "doublespeak" that cloaked his war of invasion, conquest, and coerced political allegiance in robes of morality. Government of the people, by the people and for the people did not perish from the earth when the Southern States tried to peacefully withdraw from the Union. It perished when they were driven back into it at the point of the bayonet.

The Gatekeepers of "The Lincoln Myth" guard it fiercely, for "Father Abraham, the Great Emancipator" gives to the Yankee Empire what Robert Penn Warren called a "treasury of virtue" to draw upon as it goes forth to "make the world safe for democracy." But follow the dollar and know the truth. President John F. Kennedy, for example — taking time out from his serial philandering — tried to nip Vietnam in the bud and got assassinated for it. LBJ, Brown & Root, and the rest of the Military/Industrial Complex then went on to make another killing "making Vietnam safe for democracy" while keeping the Golden Triangle open for the Mafia and the CIA's opium trade. A man who had been a Marine sniper in Vietnam saw it and wrote about it. He said Vietnam was not a war, it was an enterprise, and nine months into my own tour of duty I saw it for myself. Several weeks after I had received that gut-punch, I was riding along in a jeep one evening escorting a crippled bulldozer being carried on a lowboy tractor/trailer. Coming upon a village we saw a man standing alone and unmoving by the side of the road watching us. He was barefooted, wearing short pants, a shirt opened in the front, and a conical peasant's hat on his head. As we passed by our eyes met and he did not blink. In that one moment which I will never forget I was one of Sheridan's cavalry riding through the Shenandoah Valley.

Approaching St. Louis on Interstate 64, I saw above the skyline "The Arch" just across the Mississippi River in Missouri — "The Gateway to the West."

*

VI.

Missouri

It was on a Wednesday night, with not a star in sight,
That they robbed the Glendale Train,
And the people they did say, for many miles away,
It was robbed by Frank and Jesse James.

SOMEONE ONCE REMARKED what a coincidence it is that big rivers often run by big cities. He would have certainly found it remarkable that *two* big rivers run by St. Louis, for here is where the "Wide Missouri" empties into "The Father of Waters." In times of peak traffic on the highway through town there is a bypass at East St. Louis, Illinois, that will take you up to Interstate 70 before you cross the Mississippi River into Missouri, but coming by here in late morning on a weekday when traffic flow is fairly normal, the nice lady on my GPS usually lets me go through town on the twisting, merging and splitting myriads of Interstates. You may follow the big green signs with relative confidence, but you have to be a fast reader to do it. Crossing the mighty river and coming out of the downtown area, Interstate 64 runs through the western St. Louis metropolitan district for about twenty-five miles, crossing the Missouri River in the process, before reaching its westernmost terminus. There it merges with Interstate 70, which will take me to Kansas.

In crossing the Mississippi, one enters the lands of the old Louisiana Purchase. In 1803, Napoleon Buonaparte, Emperor of France, was in a bit of a bind. He had regained nominal ownership of the huge Louisiana Territory from the Spanish in 1800 to block the expansion of the United States at the Mississippi River. However, with France's impending war with Great Britain, her failure to put down the savage slave insurrection in San Domingo (now Haiti), and with France's financial difficulties, Napoleon offered her claims to the Trans-Mississippi watershed to the United States for $15 million. The land was mostly occupied by Native Americans and it would have to be acquired from them for settlement by treaty or conquest, but it would double the size of the Union's territories. The United States had the money to pay for it in cash, thanks to the responsible economic policies of Thomas Jefferson's administration, but President Jefferson was a strict States' Rights Constitutionalist and he questioned if the Constitution would permit the purchase. Faced with a deal too good to refuse and stretching his principled strict constructionist stance a bit, he decided that the Constitution's treaty-making power would permit it. He then appealed to the people. The Senate approved of it four to one, and the people by an even greater majority.

Jefferson then commissioned two Virginians — Meriwether Lewis and William Clark (younger brother of George Rogers Clark, who had conquered the Old Northwest Territory from the British during the Revolution) — to explore the newly acquired territory. They ascended the Missouri River to its source in the northern Rocky Mountains, crossed the mountains, and descended the Columbia River to the Pacific in what would become the Oregon Territory. The expedition was gone for two and a half years and brought back a wealth of useful information — including bones of giants to confirm the reports of contacts with giants by the early Spanish Conquistadores, and the expedition's contact with a tribe of Indians with blond hair and blue eyes that tradition said were descendants of pre-Columbian settlers from Wales. There are many segments of Meriwether Lewis' journals that are strangely missing. Perhaps the expedition discovered things that were best left buried deeply in the collections of the Smithsonian Institute. Lewis died of gunshot wounds on the Natchez Trace in 1809, leaving an intriguing mystery of whether it was murder or suicide.

In 1819, Missouri Territory applied for admission to the Union as a State. A New York congressman proposed that slavery should be prohibited before it was admitted. The Northwest Ordinance of 1787, which had prohibited slavery in the Old Northwest Territory before any States were formed, was an argument used for prohibiting slavery in Missouri, but the other side of the argument was that there had been no such prohibition on the Louisiana Purchase. Virginia furthermore argued that Congress could not arbitrarily demand that a territory alter its proposed State Constitution, for if Congress had the power to do that, then the State could lose all of its Constitutional rights to the Federal Government. (Fifty years later, during Reconstruction, Congress did just that to the Southern States with the Fourteenth Amendment.) Finally a compromise was reached. Missouri would not have to amend her Constitution to prohibit slavery, but in all future States admitted to the Union from the Louisiana Purchase above the latitude of 36 degrees 30 minutes north, slavery would be forever prohibited. Thomas Jefferson, in his retirement, said the Missouri Compromise of 1820 alarmed him "like a fire bell in the night" and filled him with dread. He considered it to be the "knell of the Union."

Settlers from the Upper South States of Virginia, North Carolina, Kentucky and Tennessee found that they could grow the familiar crops of tobacco and hemp along the Missouri River, and the region became known as "Little Dixie." These staples were shipped down the Missouri by steamboat to markets in St. Louis and further down the Mississippi, with the hemp fibers being made into bagging for cotton bales or into lines, ropes and hawsers for river or seagoing vessels. Plantations arose along the Missouri River but most of Missouri's rural inhabitants lived on small farms.

The Missouri River runs east and west through Missouri and splits the State in two. Upriver on the State's western border is Kansas City and the old steamboats would come up this far. Here was the jumping off place for the pioneers moving westward on the Oregon and the Santa Fe Trails, for the big river turns northward at this point and runs eventually to its headwaters in Montana. The Interstate crosses to the north side of the river near St. Louis in the east, back to the south side at Rocheport in the middle of the State, and brushes near it again at Kansas City. The river runs red with mud and I have seen icebergs floating down it in the dead of winter.

About seventy-five miles into the State is Kingdom City where there are truck stops, restaurants, service stations and gift shops. Fifty years ago when I was "searching for the Truth," I found myself penniless and starving with the snow coming down at Kingdom City. At a truck stop restaurant I offered to unload a man's truck for him in exchange for a meal. He said the insurance company would not let him take on any riders but that he would buy me a meal. My father once told me that if you ever get really hungry, a hot roast beef sandwich is the ticket, so that is what I ordered. When I was finished I could have eaten the same again, but when he asked if I wanted anything else I thanked that driver and said this had been a gracious plenty. I have never forgotten, so when I made the exit off of the Interstate I "paid it forward" and gave a twenty to the young man standing there with a cardboard sign. In my rambles way back then from Excelsior Springs to Columbia to Kingdom City, I always found that Missouri was filled with generous and hospitable people.

I filled up my car with gas, went to the big gift shop there called "Ozarkland" to get a little something for Mary, and then went on another twenty miles up the road to Columbia where I like to stop at an Applebee's and get a Caesar salad and a beer for lunch. A man came in and was telling the waitress that he had been sitting in stopped traffic for an hour on Interstate 70 somewhere west of town and that they were diverting westbound traffic off of the highway. When I left the restaurant, my nice AI girlfriend on the GPS directed me to a back road instead of to I-70. After a while, I crossed the empty Interstate on a two-lane overpass where the police were blocking the westbound exit ramps and I soon found myself on a two lane back road behind a string of cars sitting still. You can gamble all you want with chart plotters, Loran-C, GPS and the rest of it, but I always carry a magnetic compass in my glove compartment and a good set of charts. I broke out my trusty Road Atlas and saw where I could return to Columbia, go south to the State capital at Jefferson City, cross the Missouri there, and then get onto US 50 west to Kansas City. Being my second day on the road and a shorter drive than the first had been, I made a U-turn. The exit ramp on I-70 for eastbound traffic was open so I breezed along back to Columbia. About halfway there I saw a two lane "parking lot" over in the westbound lanes, with traffic being diverted off the highway at some exit. Everyone was standing still for miles. I didn't know how to explain to my AI girlfriend what I was doing and she was fussing at me so much that I had to cut my phone off and just follow my chart. I would get to see a whole new portion of Missouri and US 50 was four lanes, so I had a pretty good run the last hundred miles to Kansas City.

In Jackson County, on the Kansas border just south of Kansas City, US 50 passes through the town of Lone Jack. These border counties were the scene of much guerilla warfare from the days of "Bleeding Kansas" on through the War Between the States. The museum and cemetery were indicated to be right off the highway so I stopped to see what I could see. The museum was closed that day and no one was around so I walked over beneath the shade trees to the little cemetery and opened the wrought iron gate. Inside there were monuments to both Union and Confederate dead. Over where my car was parked there was a State Historical Marker telling about the battle in 1862, which was a Confederate victory. Cole Younger, who later was one of the James Gang, was in that fight. Thomas Jefferson was right: the Missouri Compromise of 1820 had been "the knell of the Union."

In my travels to the border country, I became interested in its history. As the French philosopher Voltaire observed, history is the propaganda of the victorious, so I knew I would have to take much of it with a grain of salt. One day while I was out there in Kansas, I selected a broad range of books from the "local interest" shelf at a local bookstore to try and get a true picture of things. For a balanced and concise overview, I found *Civil War in the Ozarks* by Phillip W. Steele and Steve Cottrell to be very informative. For a well-documented account of Quantrill's raid on Lawrence — devoid of all the Yankee hyperventilation over the subject — I found that Paul R. Petersen's *Quantrill at Lawrence* gave the well-documented untold story.

On the short second day of my travels west I would sometimes take a detour like this to see an historical sight. I once went to Centralia,

Missouri, to see where late in the war "Bloody Bill" Anderson's Confederate guerillas burned the depot, stopped a train, and lined up and executed thirty Union soldiers furloughed from Sherman's army in Georgia. Like the Indian troops on the border, both Union and Confederate, and like the famous mountain man Jeremiah "Liver-eating" Johnson, who served with the US 2nd Colorado Cavalry, some of Anderson's guerillas took scalps, too. Union Maj. "Ave" Johnston and his regiment of mounted infantry chased after the guerillas and were led into a trap where they were wiped out. Jesse James was credited with killing Maj. Johnston.

Taking a straight State road through farm country to Centralia, I followed the little signs from there to the battlefield south of town. I went down a tar road, then turned onto a single lane dirt farm road, and finally arrived at a grassy spot by some woods. This was evidently not part of the US Park Service. A path led me through the woods and over the creek to an open field on the other side with two markers — the Confederate marker by the woods, and the Union marker up the hill. All was quiet except for the bird calls in the green woods along the creek where the guerillas had waited in ambush on that day long ago.

Another time I took a detour to the town of Lexington, a town on the river and the scene of General Sterling Price's great victory over the Union troops in 1861. I followed the signs leading me to Lexington's Confederate Memorial Park. The park was peaceful, spacious and well-manicured, and there were several people walking about. Coming from Richmond, Virginia, I was surprised to see that no one had vandalized the sign or trashed the park. With apologies to Jason Aldean and his hit song, maybe they don't try that in a small town.

The history books divide the United States of the early nineteenth century between the "slave" States and the "free" States, but this obscures the true underlying difference between the two sections. Because of the different circumstances of geography and climate, the "free" States had evolved into an industrializing mercantile culture with small farms devoted to the raising of the cereals where slavery, once practiced there, had proven to be unprofitable, while the "slave" States remained an unchanged agrarian culture devoted to raising the staple crops of tobacco, rice and cotton. A mercantile culture consists of a financial, manufacturing and trading "core" that is dependent upon an agrarian "periphery" to provide it with raw materials for manufacturing and a market for its manufactured goods. The European powers and their colonies in the "New World" were perfect examples of a mercantile system — and of how the "core" rules the "periphery."

As the Argentine economist Raul Prebisch explained in his Dependency Theory, the price of the raw materials exported from the periphery rises more slowly than the cost of the manufactured goods that the periphery imports from the core. This eventually causes a trade imbalance in favor of the core, making the periphery a *de facto* colony instead of an equal partner. This was how Old England ruled her thirteen colonies before the Revolution, and this was how New England was threatening to rule the Southern States. The avoidance of a repetition of this situation was behind the South's determination to allow slavery in the Territories. It was considered necessary that the plantation system, and with it the South's "plantation States," expand equally in proportion to the North's "mercantile States" and not become subservient to them. Northern demagogues derided this as a diabolical effort by the so-called Southern "Slave Power" to enslave everyone, but as Tennyson wrote in his *Idylls of the King*,

And they, sweet soul, that most impute a crime

Are pronest to it, and impute themselves...

But the South was doomed from the beginning, and not just by the ever-growing power of the industrializing North with its swarms of European immigrants pouring in. Not only had the limits of the plantation system — and with it slavery— been reached in east Texas and along the Missouri River, the South's "Lost Cause" had been decreed by climate and terrain long before the first tobacco plant had ever been stuck into the ground at Jamestown.

The idea that the Federal government could prohibit slavery in the Territories was not new, as shown by the Northwest Ordinance of 1787 and the Missouri Compromise of 1820. In 1846, after Texas had been admitted to the Union as a "slave State," the Wilmot Proviso was proposed that would prohibit slavery in any more territory gained from Mexico. This Proviso was not enacted, which inflamed the Abolitionists, the Free-Soil Party, and finally the Republicans — the party of the Northern mercantile interests and the first purely sectional party in American history to gain national political power. The Compromise of 1850 cooled passions briefly when California was admitted as a "free State" and the Fugitive Slave Law was strengthened, but the Kansas-Nebraska Act of 1854 lit the fires of "Bleeding Missouri" and "Bleeding Kansas."

The Act allowed the territories of Kansas and Nebraska to be organized, and it allowed the settlers themselves to determine whether or not slavery would be allowed in their territories. Since both territories were above the latitude of 36 degrees 30 minutes north, the Act would negate the Missouri Compromise of 1820. Missouri settlers moved into eastern Kansas to stake claims and try to set up a pro-slavery territorial government, but Massachusetts Abolitionists formed the Emigrant Aid Society and rushed people and guns to Kansas to set up their own government and make Kansas "Free Soil for Free Men." Conflict soon broke out in Kansas that devolved into bloody raids back and forth across the border between Kansas "Jayhawkers" and Missouri "Border Ruffians." Kansas Jayhawkers stole Missouri slaves, sometimes sending them north on the Underground Railroad and sometimes returning the slaves they had stolen back to Missouri to collect the reward money for "runaways."

When the War Between the States broke out, Kansas was admitted to the Union as a "free State," while Missouri tried a neutrality that didn't last long. Governor Claiborne Jackson described Lincoln's call for troops illegal and unconstitutional and began drilling State militia near St. Louis. Captain Nathaniel Lyon with several thousand US Army troops marched out of St. Louis, surrounded the militia encampment, captured some, and dispersed the rest; but when he marched those he had captured back through town as prisoners of war he was attacked by mobs. When shots were fired and several soldiers fell, the troops fired on the crowd, killing a number of civilians. St. Louis was heavily populated by strongly pro-Union

German immigrants, and the next day a thousand German troops in Union uniforms were attacked by mobs and the bloodshed continued. These German soldiers, some of whom could not speak English, were looked upon by Southerners the same way as the Hessian mercenaries hired by the English during the Revolutionary War were looked upon by the colonists — foreigners meddling in something that was none of their business.

When Lyon, a friend of Abraham Lincoln, was made a Brigadier General he declared war on Missouri. Governor Jackson appointed General Sterling Price as commander of the Missouri State Militia. Lyon took his US Army troops up the Missouri River to capture the capital at Jefferson City while Jackson, Price and their State Militia abandoned the capital and withdrew southwestward towards Arkansas to link up with the Confederate Army. Lyon pursued and was met by Price at Wilson's Creek where Lyon was killed and his army defeated. Missouri then seceded and was given the twelfth star in the Confederate Flag. Price pushed back northward to the Missouri River, captured Lexington, and then returned south again for the winter. In the following early spring Price and other Confederate armies were defeated at Elkhorn Tavern in northwestern Arkansas, and Missouri was under heavy Union occupation thereafter. Except for Price's raid in 1864, guerrilla warfare raged across the State for the rest of the war.

The most successful of the Confederate guerrillas were William Clarke Quantrill and his Raiders. Among their nemeses were the marauding and freebooting 7th Kansas Cavalry, known as "Jennison's Jayhawkers," and the wild-haired fanatical Kansas Senator Jim Lane and his "Lane's Brigade," for he was another favorite of President Lincoln and was given a commission as a Brigadier General. In late summer of 1861, Lane and his brigade rode into Missouri to punish anyone who had offered aid to General Price's troops. He left a trail of burning destruction comparable in wantonness to Sherman's march through Georgia and the Carolinas. In September 1861, he burned the town of Osceola, Missouri, to the ground. How many homes he plundered and burned, no one knows. Age made no difference to the Kansas Jayhawkers or the hated Kansas Redlegs (a group of ardent

Abolitionists who were distinguished by the red leggings that they wore); old men were strung up and young boys were shot down.

In the beginning Quantrill's men were mostly acting as State Guards, not "Bushwhackers," trying to protect the people from the depredations of the Jayhawkers, but in 1862, Quantrill made two retaliatory raids into Kansas, one to Aubry in retaliation for the burnings of Columbus and Dayton, Missouri by the radical Kansas Abolitionist Daniel Anthony, brother of the suffragette Susan B. Anthony, and another to Olathe in revenge for the execution by firing squad at Ft. Leavenworth of one of his captured men after Quantrill had offered a prisoner exchange.

Confederate "Bushwhackers" raided Union outposts and ambushed Union patrols while Union retaliations were made against the civilian population suspected of harboring the Bushwhackers. In 1863, General Thomas Ewing, brother-in-law to General William T. Sherman, ordered Union troops to arrest nine Missouri women on the western border on charges of spying and aiding Bushwhackers. The women were imprisoned on the second floor of a three-story brick building in Kansas City, with one of the girls having a ball and chain attached to her leg. Federal troops on the first floor in the adjoining building being used as a guardhouse removed some partitions between the buildings, including the support for the second floor, in order to visit some "fallen women" who were imprisoned on the first floor. This caused both buildings to collapse, killing four of the young women imprisoned above and injuring others. Was it premeditated murder by Kansas Jayhawkers? With nothing known at the time to refute the allegation, and since the Yankees were now making war on their womenfolk, the Missouri guerrillas thought it was, and they were infuriated. Three of Cole Younger's sisters and two of his cousins had been incarcerated there. One of his cousins was killed and so was the sister of another member of Quantrill's Raiders. Fourteen year old Josephine Anderson was killed, her older sister, Mary Ellen, was crippled and disfigured for life, and her younger sister, ten year old Janie, suffered two broken legs, an injured back, and a lacerated face. They were the three sisters of one of Quantrill's Captains named Bill Anderson. At the news he went berserk and became the pathological

Yankee-killer who came to be known as "Bloody Bill" Anderson. His tally cord, found on his body after he was killed, had over fifty knots in it. Two weeks later Quantrill and his infuriated Raiders made their bloody raid on Lawrence, Kansas, the hotbed of Kansas Jayhawkers and Abolitionists.

Cole Younger said that the Lawrence Raid was one of the most misrepresented events of the war. Facts that were ignored or downplayed were that it was a viable military target as a Northern recruiting center, and that it housed a vast amount of military stores and supplies. Not only was it a Union garrison, it was also the headquarters of the hated Kansas "Redlegs" and the base of operations for the Jayhawkers, where loot from Missouri homes was auctioned off to Kansas homemakers. Although the lurid tales of political propaganda now would have one to believe it was a murderous raid on innocent civilians, in fact, Quantrill's Raiders directed their operations against the military targets and the militia stationed there — and against wanted men. Women and children were not harmed.

Lists of wanted men and the location of their residences had been provided to Quantrill by a spy he had sent there before the raid. Senator Jim Lane — the notorious looter and burner of Missouri homes — was an especially wanted man, but he escaped by hiding in a corn field and Quantrill's men had to be satisfied with burning down his house. After the Lawrence Raid, General Ewing issued his notorious General Order No. 11, ordering the citizens of four counties on the western Missouri border to vacate the district, leaving a barren and empty landscape.

The war on the border was different than the war in the East. In Virginia, between two capitals a hundred miles apart, great armies clashed, with casualties often numbering well into the thousands. Seventeen thousand men were killed in one day at Sharpsburg, and in the Overland Campaign from The Wilderness to Cold Harbor, Grant lost sixty thousand men — more men than Lee had in his whole army at the outset of the campaign. But the war in Missouri was near the frontier, where Confederate Indians and Texas Rangers fought side by side, where Kansas Redlegs and Jayhawkers gave no quarter to Bushwhackers and civilians alike in their raids on Missouri, where the Missouri guerrillas raised the Black Flag in retaliation, and where ambushes and raids might tally five or ten casualties and where a notable fight might tally forty or a hundred. It became a war of the feud and the vendetta.

Frank James served at Wilson's Creek with General Price. When the army withdrew into Arkansas, he was left in a hospital with measles where he was captured and paroled. He returned home to Clay County, but with the continuing depredations being made by the Jayhawkers in Missouri, he joined Quantrill. Jayhawkers came to his home looking for him. They repeatedly hung Dr. Rueben Samuel, his stepfather, to try and make him reveal where Frank was, and left him hanging when he wouldn't tell. Frank's mother Zerelda cut him down before he died, but his brain had been starved of oxygen for so long that he was mentally impaired for the rest of his life. Frank's young brother Jesse was out plowing when the Jayhawkers showed up and gave him a bull-whipping when he wouldn't talk, either. Afterwards, Jesse lied about his age and joined Quantrill. He was a crack shot with a pistol. It was said that he could shoot the head off of a chicken while he was riding a horse at a full gallop. He was a fearless fighter and he earned the respect of the Raiders.

Jesse and Frank James rode with "Bloody Bill" Anderson and were at the Centralia massacre in September 1864. In October, Anderson was killed, Jesse went to Texas for the winter, and Frank went to Kentucky with Quantrill. When Quantrill was killed there in early 1865, Frank surrendered and was paroled.

In the spring of 1865, the Confederate Armies surrendered, and the war was over. Jesse came back to Missouri to take the surrender terms offered to the guerrillas, but he was shot coming into town while holding a white flag. Bitter at the treatment he and his family had received, and proscribed along with other ex-Confederates during Reconstruction, Jesse took to the outlaw trail. With his brother Frank, and with Bob, Jim and Cole Younger, they robbed Yankee owned or operated banks and railroads. In 1882, Robert Ford shot Jesse James in the back for the reward money, but he left a legend that will not die.

*

VII.

Kansas

John Brown's body lies a moldering in the grave

But his soul goes marching on...

IF ONE SHOULD EVER WISH to see the prototypical image of a fanatical New England Puritan, go to the Kansas Statehouse in Topeka. There you will see a painting of one towering over embroiled humanity like one of those colossal wind turbines on the High Plains that towers over a little farming community like an angry, alien god stirring it to madness. He is wild-eyed with a broad white beard blowing over his shoulder, and his mouth is wide open like he is some blasphemous impersonator of God Almighty bellowing judgment, hellfire and damnation onto sinful mortals. His arms are stretched wide in the image of an old rugged cross, but though he was "martyred" with a hangman's noose at Charles Town, Virginia, in 1859, he is no crucified Savior, and the blood on his hands (carefully not depicted by the artist) does not come from Roman spikes. It comes from the murders he committed on Pottawatomie Creek and at Harpers Ferry; and not only from these, but from the slave insurrection he had tried and failed to instigate that led to the bloodiest war in the history of the Western Hemisphere; for slavery was a dying institution all over the industrializing world in the nineteenth century until the radical Abolitionists brought the natural progress of emancipation here to an abrupt halt with their fanatical attempts to drench the South in the blood of another San Domingo. Their incessant and rabid attempts drove the South to separate from the Union for self-preservation at the election of their radical Abolitionist party in 1860. But their party was also the party of the North's avaricious "Mercantile Kingdom" which wanted to control the South's "Cotton Kingdom," so it blockaded the Southern coast and sent its invading armies marching across the South singing "John Brown's Body" and "The Battle Hymn of the Republic" while burning, plundering, raping and killing their way from the Potomac to the Rio Grande. That blood is also on his hands.

Perennial Utopian fanatics, on their crusades "to make a better world" and forever claiming to be "on the right side of history," are blinded by their hubris to the fact that history is not a linear march towards a Utopian dream, but a cyclic march of folly where Utopian dreams are turned into totalitarian nightmares. They are Robespierre with his guillotines and his Reign of Terror shouting "Liberty, Equality, Fraternity"; they are the Radical Abolitionists with their genocidal Crusade against Southern White people singing "Glory, Glory Hallelujah!," they are the Bolshevik Lenin, the Socialist Hitler (yes, of the National *Socialist* German Workers' Party), the Communist Stalin and the Marxist Mao, all with their untold millions murdered, tortured or sent to the gulags, the concentration camps, or the gas chambers to "make a better world" by getting rid of the "enemies of the people."

Looking closely at this painting of John Brown by John Steuart Curry you will see in his wild hair the shape of two horns rising up out of the top of his head. This is Baphomet incarnate whose "soul goes marching on," inspiring the raging "social justice warriors" of today to obliterate all monuments, all art, all books, and all of the records of history that would indict them for the reigns of terror and the murders of millions that their kind have offered down through the ages as a blood-sacrifice to Satan "to make a better world."

John Randolph of Roanoke once asked of the Radical Abolitionists, "Who made thee, Cain, thy brother's keeper?" Who, indeed...

*

VIII.

Beyond

Where dips the rocky highland
Of Sleuth Wood in the lake,
There lies a leafy island
Where flapping herons wake
The drowsy water-rats;
There we've hid our faery vats,
Full of berries
And of reddest stolen cherries.
Come away, O human child!
To the waters and the wild
With a faery, hand in hand,
For the world's more full of weeping than you can understand... — W. B. Yeats

A MILE OR TWO DOWN A DUSTY gravel road one turns into a neatly maintained drive of another quarter-mile length. It is bordered by well-trimmed grass and wire fencing, beyond which is the tall flowering prairie grass. As one approaches the gate to the ranch, one is met by a cacophony of dogs leaping and barking to greet the latest visitor. Scooby, the bad boy, jumps the fence like a deer. Prolo, my bonded friend and getting a bit porky these days, leaps like a puppy. I hold the gate closely when I enter so the crowd doesn't slip out. Fiona, my Siberian Ice Queen, runs and leans herself against my leg. I ask my true love if she has been faithful to me while I have been gone, or has she perhaps been seeing someone else? No confessions are forthcoming, but coyly she allows me to scratch her stomach. Destiny, the sweet fluffy matron and stepmother of big Ben and Beatrice, comes and licks my arm as I scratch her ruff. She is sweet and demure but, like Germany, she is always picking fights and losing them. Orville and Wilbur, both with rickets and gimpy hind legs, come up to greet me, as does that rascal Ranger, the full-grown but still rambunctious puppy. New additions greet me as well, some barking behind their fenced-in yards. Big Charlie surveys the domain calmly from his enclosure by the detached garage, as a cloud of little fluffy ones come pouring out of the house when Mary comes to welcome me.

I unload my things from the car and carry them into the apartment which is attached to the Morton building that houses the equipment bays, the racks of dog food stacked on pallets, and more kennels in the back. Mary takes me on a late afternoon ride around the ranch in the Gator to show me the big pond down across the mowed pasture, while the dogs chase us with joy at the excitement of a run. Swallows dip and play with the dogs, who joyfully and futilely chase the birds around in their aerobatic circles.

When evening comes, I offer to fix something for supper from the apartment galley from some groceries I have purchased before my arrival, and we make something light to eat. We take our meal at the table out on the deck by the apartment, with a half-dozen dogs for company, and sit watching the sunset over the prairie. It is a pleasure to sit out here "of an evening" as our grandmother would say, listening to the fountain raining into the little pond in the copse of cottonwood trees nearby, where a heron flaps its wings coming in for the night. The sun sets directly across from us now, but as the year wanes it will work its way back south to our left. As the radiant sun sets, the sliver of a moon follows it down and all is still. As the stars come out one by one, we talk quietly about the morrow.

With volunteers arriving in the morning to help tend to the dogs, Mary and I get into the car and head west. After passing through the rolling green Flint Hills we come to the open flat lands that herald the transition from the prairies to the plains. After an hour we turn off the Interstate and take the long, straight back roads of western Kansas until we arrive at a small farm town and a little country church. There we hear the Word of God. Then we follow in procession to the cemetery where I help to carry a friend back to the soil from whence he came — the broad farmlands verging on the immensity of the High Plains, which, like the sea, "receives no impress, preserves no memories, and keeps no reckoning of lives."

*

About The Author

A NATIVE OF LYNCHBURG, Virginia, H. V. Traywick, Jr., graduated from the Virginia Military Institute in 1967 with a degree in Civil Engineering and a Regular Commission in the US Army. His service included qualification as an Airborne Ranger and command of an Engineer company in Vietnam where he received the Bronze Star. After his return, he resigned his commission and ended by making a career as a tugboat captain. During this time, he was able to earn a Master of Liberal Arts from the University of Richmond with an international focus on war and cultural revolution. He is a member of The Jamestowne Society, The Society of the Cincinnati in the State of Virginia, The Sons of Confederate Veterans, The Society of Independent Southern Historians, and a past member of the VMI Board of Visitors He currently lives in Richmond where he writes, studies history, and occasionally commutes to Norfolk to serve as a tugboat pilot.

Latest Releases & Best Sellers

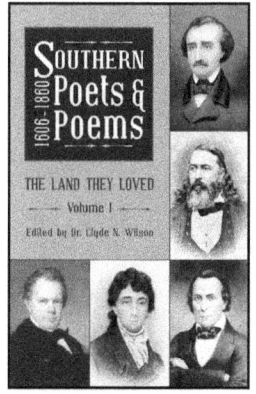
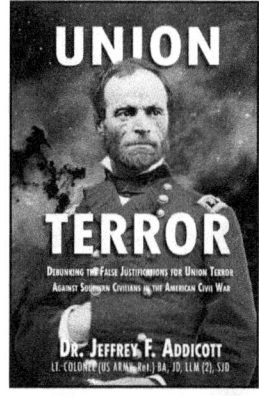

OVER 70 UNAPOLOGETICALLY
SOUTHERN TITLES FOR YOU TO ENJOY

SHOTWELLPUBLISHING.COM

Free Book Offer

DON'T GET LEFT OUT, Y'ALL.
Sign-up and be the first to know about new releases, sales, and other goodies
—plus we'll send you TWO FREE EBOOKS!

Lies My Teacher Told Me:
The True History of the War for
Southern Independence
by Dr. Clyde N. Wilson

When The Yankees Come
Former Carolina Slaves Remember
Sherman's March From the Sea
by Paul C. Graham

FreeLiesBook.com

Southern Books. No Apologies.
We love the South — its history,
traditions, and culture — and are proud
of our inheritance as Southerners.
Our books are a reflection of this love.

www.ingramcontent.com/pod-product-compliance
Lightning Source LLC
Chambersburg PA
CBHW070654050426
42451CB00008B/352